GET THIS FR

Limited Time Offer

FREE

The Research Behind This Book That You Are Now Reading

By Brian Godawa

100 pages of biblical and historical sources with citations, proving the fulfillment of each verse in Matthew 24. PDF format.

http://godawa.com/matthew-24/

Are We Living in the Last Days?

Check out this Controversial Online Course!

25% OFF!

Limited Time Only

10+ Intense Lectures on End Times

Powerpoint Videos with Powerful Visuals By Brian Godawa

There are so many Christians teaching outrageous things about Bible Prophecy these days. It's enough to frustrate the serious Bible student. What would you think if you found out most all of it is simply mistaken? What if you found out that the ancient mindset of the Jewish writers was influenced by the Old Testament imagery of the past, and not a crystal ball gaze into our modern future? What if you found out that everything that modern prophecy pundits are looking for—the antichrist, the Beast, the Tribulation, the Rapture—was not what they told you it was, but something different?

Includes lots of colorful and helpful PowerPoint visuals, charts, pictures, and film clips for a much richer presentation of the material.

PLUS a bunch of FREE Bonuses!

Check out the Free Introduction & Learn More
(Use Code NTBA84 for 25% Discount)

Click Here
For Details

LastDaysCourse.com

End Times Bible Prophecy

It's Not What They Told You

By Brian Godawa

End Times Bible Prophecy: It's Not What They Told You
1st Edition

Copyright © 2017, Brian Godawa
All rights reserved. No part of this book may be reproduced in any form or by any electronic or mechanical means, including information storage and retrieval systems, without prior written permission, except in the case of brief quotations in critical articles and reviews.

Embedded Pictures Publishing
Los Angeles, CA
310.948.0224
www.embeddedpictures.com

ISBN: 978-1-942858-31-7 (paperback)
ISBN: 978-1-942858-32-4 (ebook)

Scripture quotations are taken from *The Holy Bible: English Standard Version*. Wheaton: Standard Bible Society, 2001, except where noted as the NASB95: *New American Standard Bible: 1995 Update*. (LaHabra, CA: The Lockman Foundation, 1995).

Dedicated to
Michael Gavlak

Special thanks to my wife Kimberly for her perpetually loving support, to Doug Van Dorn for his constructive criticism, and to Bette Smyth for her proofreading.

Table of Contents

Preface
Please Read This. It's Important.

Writing about Bible prophecy and the end times is a very tricky thing. The study of end things is called *eschatology*, and many people tend to be very invested in their eschatological beliefs. When those beliefs are challenged, one is often met with hostility and broken fellowship. Those most committed to their views have spent long hours, sometimes many years, studying their particular view. Many prophecy writers and ministers have committed their lives and incomes to encouraging their followers to keep the faith in their interpretation. There is a lot of money being made in the commercial world of end times Bible prophecy. Those heavily invested would risk losing their reputations, audiences, and incomes if they changed their views or seriously considered other interpretations. Because of this entrenchment, open mindedness is not often rewarded in the world of Bible prophecy. Minority viewpoints are easily dismissed and frequently slandered as heresy.

Can't We All Get Along?

I know—I've been in that position. I studied the Scriptures with diligence for years in search of answers to the questions about the last days. I ended up changing my eschatology several times during those years. I'll tell you that story in chapter 1. But right now, I want to let you know that I am very aware that I am going to be treading on "sacred ground" for some of you. I want to be as respectful as I can. I have the desire only to address issues, not attack individuals. Because of that, I will not be making many references to specific authors, other than those relevant to my personal story or illustrative of a point.

The first half of my book focuses on proper Bible interpretation (hermeneutics), apart from any eschatological view. I explore how to understand biblical symbols, poetry, and literal versus figurative language in prophecy by interpreting the text within its ancient Hebrew context as the original writers intended. The goal is to read it through the eyes of an ancient Jew steeped in the Law and the Prophets, not a modern Westerner steeped in Twitter and online news trends. I will not be arguing for any specific view of the end times at that point. So no matter what view you have, you should have few problems with it. All views should be able to find common ground.

The Sensational Search for Significance

There is another sad aspect of eschatology these days that troubles me. It seems that the most sensational interpretations get the most "likes" and views on social media and increase the potential for making money. YouTubers, bloggers and podcasters are pressured into making fantastic claims, or they risk losing views and attention. Conspiracy theories abound and Christians are often the most gullible, being baited with what amounts to science fiction. They want more than mere Christian faith in their lives; they want to *experience* the supernatural. Don't we all? They want proof that the Bible is true and that they are in the right. Bible prophecy gives them that affirmation. If we are living in the last days, if Bible prophecy is being fulfilled right before our very eyes, then our eyes give us that empirical certainty that our faith longs for. We are right. Yes, we have to be right. It's happening right before our eyes!

It also gives us perceived significance. If we are participating in the last days, then we are the last generation, the climax of God's timetable before the Second Coming. If these are not the last days, then we are just another generation of Christians who live and die without that particular significance we crave.

But we want to be important to God, even more important than all those who suffered and died in silence throughout the millennia. They were not the special generation that participated in anything other than living their Christian lives faithfully and spreading the gospel of the kingdom of God.

How our priorities have become corrupted.

Open Eyes, Open Minds

Yes, I do have a specific eschatology, and I will try to explain that in the second half of the book as I give a brief exegesis of the Olivet Discourse of Jesus. I am open to other interpretations and changing my mind. I could be wrong. I've been wrong before. None of us has arrived at perfection. We Christians should always be humbly learning and adjusting our views as we grow spiritually. I have believed in all the major systems of eschatology throughout my life, and the only thing I am certain of is that they are all imperfect. They all have holes, anomalies, and weaknesses. My goal is to follow the truth wherever it leads me, even if it means giving up my cherished beliefs. So my goal is to follow the eschatology that has the least amount of holes and anomalies, the one that explains the most Scripture within its original, ancient context and intent—of which we will never have absolute certainty. In my opinion those who tell us that we can be certain are fundamentally wrong.

We walk by faith, not by sight (2 Cor 5:7). We are significant to God, not because the Antichrist may be alive in our generation, but because Jesus *is* alive through all generations!

Brian Godawa

If you find this book helpful or interesting, be sure to check out my novel series *Chronicles of the Apocalypse* which incarnates this eschatology in a dramatic, fictional narrative of the historical events.

PART ONE
Why Prophecy Matters

Chapter 1
My Journey to the End of the World

I became a Christian in high school in the 1970s through a non-denominational church. It had basic evangelical goals: introducing the unchurched to Jesus Christ and building their fellowship. They avoided controversies as well as the nonessential doctrinal distinctions of denominations. My only concern was to share the wonderful good news that I had learned that freed me from a burdened life of trying to save myself through my good works. Based on the shed blood of Jesus on the cross for my sins, I was saved by grace, through faith, and that not of myself; it was a gift of God. That was pretty much all I knew, and that was pretty much all that mattered.

When I went to college my Christian roommate discipled me, and I grew in my faith and understanding of the Scriptures. I caught a vision for the "lost." I became fueled with the desire to introduce others to Jesus Christ so that they too could find the forgiveness of sins that I had and come into a right relationship with their Creator. The gospel was for everyone. I began to learn the finer points of biblical doctrine and theology as well as the importance of a Christian worldview—a comprehensive way of seeing the world that informed my choices and actions.

The Beginning of the End

And then I read Hal Lindsey's *The Late Great Planet Earth.* Most people today are familiar with the wildly successful 1990s *Left Behind* fiction series that made end times Bible prophecy a topic of interest even in the mainstream secular world. Well, *Left Behind* wasn't the first to do so, and it wasn't even the most popular. That series of sixteen best-selling novels has sold more than sixty-five million copies and had dominated the New York Times best-sellers list for years. But *The Late Great Planet Earth* was one single book by Hal Lindsey, and it sold twenty-eight million copies alone by the time *Left Behind* came out. Hal Lindsey's material literally changed the landscape of evangelical eschatology (the study of end things—remember that word, *eschatology*. It's important). Of course he wasn't the first to do so either. The belief system that Lindsey promoted is called *dispensationalism*, and that theology began in the early 1800s. But the point is that *Late Great* was immensely popular, greatly influential, and it changed my life.

Reading his book I was introduced to a new paradigm of Christianity. I no longer saw my existence on this planet as merely a Christian with a message of liberation for spiritual captives and a biblical blueprint for the reformation of our lawless secular culture. Rather, I saw myself as a Christian smack dab in the middle of the climax of history, one minute before midnight on the prophetic clock before all hell broke loose and Jesus returned to judge the world. Lindsey taught me that everything that was happening in the world around me had actually been foretold in the Bible. How exciting! But also, how urgent! I discovered a new aspect of the gospel message that included prophetic judgment on the world as a reason to repent and get right with God.

Lindsey's eschatology was (and still is) centered around the nation state of Israel and the Jewish people. I had always treasured the story of Israel in the Old Testament and how it led up to the coming Messiah, Jesus. The Jews were God's chosen people, but they rejected their Messiah. So Jesus opened his kingdom to all who would believe, both Jew and Gentile, with the new covenant. The ancient Hebrews and their geopolitical nation were part of my spiritual heritage in the old covenant, but not the focus of the new covenant of faith in Christ.

Lindsey introduced me to the idea that the Jews were still God's chosen people and continued to remain at the center of God's plan. The church of Jesus Christ was an historical parenthesis, or a temporary break from God's dealings with the Jews. Yes, the church was important to God now, but only until he restarted that prophetic time clock to initiate the end of history when he would fulfill his promises to the Jews of Israel. In effect, there are two peoples of God—the church and Israel—but Israel was the original and irrevocable chosen nation. It was all about the geopolitical state of Israel.

This seemed to make sense to me. After all, the Middle East was embattled, as it always seems to be, and this made sense of all the irrational anti-Semitism of Israel's Arab and Muslim neighbors. Didn't God predict that the offspring of Ishmael would forever be at enmity with the offspring of Isaac? It seemed to explain why the Jews, after millennia of persecution, still managed to survive as a people and miraculously regain their homeland in 1948. It was clear to me that there was something special about Israel, something *chosen*.

According to Lindsey, this reforming of the nation state of Israel was the lynchpin to the whole prophetic system. Every generation in history has had its share of false prophets predicting the end of the world. But never before had the catalyst for the end of days been in place. That catalyst was Israel becoming a nation in 1948 with the approval of the United Nations. Didn't Jesus say that his physical second coming would take place within a generation of all the things he prophesied in Matthew 24? So Lindsey concluded,

> What generation? Obviously, in context, the generation that would see the signs—chief among them, the rebirth of Israel. A generation in the Bible is something like 40 years. If this is a correct deduction, then within forty years or so of 1948, all these things could take place.[1]

Wow! It was now the 1980s and the final countdown to Armageddon was ticking away. I would be in the generation that would see the second coming of Jesus Christ. Well, not really. Actually we Christians would be the generation that would be protected from God's wrath because we would be raptured to heaven before the final series of God's judgments came on the earth. Jesus could come at any moment. We just had to be ready or we would be left behind to endure that wrath. Most everyone nowadays knows about the rapture—the removal of believers from earth to heaven. Even the secular world has made a TV series about it. But not back then. Back then it was a secret mystery that primarily sparked the imaginations and hope of millions of Christians. After that rapture, a period of seven years called the great

---

[1] Hal Lindsey, *The Late Great Planet Earth* (Grand Rapids, MI: Zondervan, 1970-1971), 54.

tribulation would occur with a series of events surrounding the Antichrist—the incarnation of Satan as a false messiah of the world, an evil mirror image of Christ.

Bible Prophecy Charts Galore

Lindsey and others had proven to me that the Antichrist was "alive and well on planet earth," expanding his power and influence to be soon revealed. He would deceive the world into thinking he was bringing peace; he would make a treaty with Israel and rebuild the temple in Jerusalem. But then he would break that treaty, set up a statue of himself in the temple, proclaim himself to be god, and give everyone the mark of the Beast. God would commence with all kinds of judgments on the earth as depicted in the book of Revelation—earthquakes, plagues, famines—unlike anything in the history of the world. This Beast would ultimately join with a ten-nation confederacy to invade Israel in the final battle of Armageddon against God's people. But of course Jesus would return at that battle, destroy Satan and all his minions, and establish a thousand-year reign on earth.

There are many more details of course, but that was the basic scenario. And, with minor exceptions, that storyline still exists today in the world of popular Bible prophecy. I memorized the Bible prophecy chart and told unbelievers that Jesus was coming soon and that there wasn't much time to get right with God. It was an exciting time to be alive, to read the newspapers and see the unfolding of Bible prophecy. It seemed that every week something happened in the news that Bible prophecy teachers explained to me were fulfillment or setups for fulfillment of the last days. And it seemed pretty self-evident. I mean the world was getting worse and worse. Abortion on demand was murdering a million or more babies a year. Society was getting more immoral and more intolerant of Christianity. As America rejected its Christian heritage, it was going to hell in a handbasket. We were rearranging the deck chairs on the Titanic. I even had a friend whose family was not bothering to send their kids to college, since Jesus would probably return before it mattered anyway.

I thought that was a little extreme. But the urgency was part of the message. And I felt my God-commanded duty to preach it more and more. And I studied the Bible in light of the newspaper in order to show myself approved—a Berean, as the Bible called me. It was invigorating to my faith. I was getting the confirmation, the verification that my faith longed for. After all, if Bible prophecy was right in its predictions, then that proved it was God's Word. Bible prophecy of the first coming of Christ persuaded those who believed, so Bible prophecy of the second coming of Christ would persuade more to follow Jesus.

You Mean There's Another Way?

But then something happened. I found out that all this material that I had learned about the end times was just one interpretation of Bible prophecy, but it wasn't the only possible interpretation. Not only that, it was actually one of the newer views of eschatology called *dispensationalism*. I had never heard that before. I had thought what Lindsey and others were doing was simply reading the plain language of the Bible, as if there was really no other legitimate approach. Bible prophecy was either true or false, but I never realized that there were entire systems of interpretation at odds with the dispensationalism of *Late Great Planet Earth*.

When I heard that a different system of interpretation called *historic premillennialism* denied the centrality of geopolitical Israel, I was shocked. When I found out that *amillennialism* interpreted many prophecies as figurative and poetic, I thought, "Only liberals don't take the Bible literally." And when I heard that there was a school of interpretation called *preterism* that considers last days prophecies to have been fulfilled in the first century of the new covenant, I thought, "Heresy!" *Futurism* (another term to remember in this book), is the belief that last-days prophesies are still in our future. Futurism had to be the only way to understand the Bible or you were denying the second coming of Christ!

But then I learned that all these other views had valid theological defenders who were godly, orthodox Christian scholars. And these views had been there through most of church history. Dispensational teachers dismissed other views, as if to protect their followers from being influenced by them.

But I felt betrayed by the dishonesty, not protected. Why would these other views be treated with such disrespect when they were the dominant views in church history until recent times? Majority views do not make something true, neither does the age of a view, nor the first in line. But that truth plays both ways. Just because the dominant view of Bible prophecy was currently this new dispensational view, that fact didn't make it more true either. So I launched into the study of these various eschatological views because I wanted to be educated, not propagandized.

Everything Keeps Changing

Something else was occurring in my outlook. As the years went on, I noticed that these Bible prophecy teachers kept finding fulfilled Bible prophecies in each and every major geopolitical news event that was occurring. If you charted the radio shows, books, newsletters, blogposts and podcasts over the past fifty years, you would find manifold more fulfillments of Bible prophecies than there are actual Bible prophesies—and more altered predictions than any of them would like to admit. I saw that as the geopolitical scene changed, these prognostications would change, adjusted to fit the new "proof of Bible prophecy."

In the 1970s, Islamic political involvement was virtually unknown on the world scene, and we heard almost nothing about Islam from prophecy pundits. Now, Islam plays heavily in the futurist prophecy scenario, some even saying the Antichrist will be Islamic. In the 1970s, the European Common Market (ECM) was about to get its tenth member to become the ten-nation confederacy against Israel, allegedly spoken of in Revelation and Daniel (Rev 12:3; 17:3; Dan 7:7). Later, the ECM had sixteen members and ultimately dissolved, so that interpretation had to be replaced by other "fulfillments." But just because a viewpoint may have been wrong about some things in the past doesn't mean it is wrong about all things now. Logically that is true. But if a system keeps changing its interpretations, doesn't that imply an inherent problem with the system and/or its interpreters?

Most prophecy pundits avoid making hard predictions because they know the punishment for false prophets in the Old Testament was death (Deut 18:20-22). Of course the Old Testament is not applied in today's church culture, but the principle remains that false prophets are condemned with the harshest of judgment. For all their belief in literally interpreting the Bible, prophecy pundits never quite say literally what they are predicting. They use hedging terms like *could be* and *maybe*, or they ask leading questions like, "Could this be what the prophet foretold?" or "It is very likely that . . . " But making a myriad of implied predictions without direct claims is still making predictions.

Some of these nonprophetic prophesies have become too clearly wrong to deny. Lindsey made a documentary movie based on his book by the same title, *The Late Great Planet Earth*, using the dark and forebodingly authoritative voice of Orson Welles as narrator. In that movie he reaffirmed that the key to the whole prophetic pattern "has always been the rebirth of the state of Israel." But he also made startling doomsday predictions as the birth pangs Jesus spoke of signaling his soon return. He claimed that the Jupiter Effect that was to happen in his near future of 1982 would involve the lining up of planets that would cause catastrophes on earth. He interviewed Paul Ehrlich of *The Population Bomb* fame who predicted that "by 2014, we would have 8 billion people, but we're probably going to have a huge die off before we get there." Ehrlich also claimed that "our natural resources will be exhausted by the year 2000." Ehrlich also claimed in 1974 that the earth would soon be frozen over by global cooling in a new ice age. Now he says the world will be burned up by global warming within our lifetimes.[2] Lindsey showed images of Ted Kennedy, Ronald Reagan, and Jimmy Carter, while clearly implying that one of them could be the Antichrist (That movie can be seen in its entirety on YouTube). It wasn't until decades later that the absurdity of these predictions were evident. But by then Lindsey's devotees had long forgotten the false prophesies and supported his new predictions. I saw through the years that he continued to be wrong over and over again. Yet to this day he is still a noted Bible prophecy teacher.

Back in 1980, Lindsey's not-so-subtle prediction that Christ would return by 1988 was exciting and inspiring, even hopeful. Now, almost two generations later than his "generation prediction," thirty years past his deadline, that lynchpin devastates his entire system based as it was on the supposedly central prophecy of Israel's national statehood. But many still teach this dispensational scheme, including the writings of the late *Left*

[2] https://realclimatescience.com/2015/11/before-he-was-pushing-the-global-warming-scam-paul-ehrlich-was-pushing-the-global-cooling-scam/

Behind author Tim LaHaye. In order to maintain the legitimacy of the system, they reinterpreted a generation to be eighty years; and now it is a hundred years. They just keep stretching the years to keep the system plausible. These prophecy teachers are still talking the same way today they did fifty years ago, but what they are calling fulfilled prophecy is completely different from what they originally maintained. They just keep changing it to fit the news.

The More Things Change, the More They Stay the Same

I don't have anything personal against Lindsey or LaHaye. The eschatology of *Late Great* was simply the narrative that I personally wrestled with over those years. This was my journey. But it all applies by analogy to today. Many modern Bible prophecy teachers are promoting the same system of interpretation with newly adjusted "fulfilled" prophecies and dire predictions to fit the current era. Sure, there are minor differences, but the big picture is still the same futuristic scenario of a revived Roman empire, the rapture at some point in time, the Antichrist, the mark of the Beast, the great tribulation, and geopolitical Israel's centrality to God's plan. Bible prophecies are still being "fulfilled before our very eyes" every week on prophecy podcasts and blogs, just like in the 1970s. Sadly, as I indicated earlier, the more sensational these claims, the more viral they become, creating a kind of Bible prophecy industrial complex. The storytellers have changed but the narrative remains the same.

It is not my goal to mock these prophecy failures. I am not going to name names and attack individual pundits in this book. Some of you may be following these individuals and their teachings. I don't want to insult you or put you on the defensive. I want to address *ideas* not *people* and focus on God's Word, not man's newspapers. I want to let the Scriptures speak for themselves within their original, ancient Hebrew context. Like most of you, I believe that God's Word is true and that whatever he prophesies to happen will happen. The question is what was God actually prophesying? Prophecies are often poetic, visionary and cryptic. Metaphors and symbols abound in the ancient Hebrew worldview. Could we have misunderstood what God was saying in the text? Is it possible that we have imported our own context onto the text, creating a pretext? These are the questions I began to ask myself as I studied other views of the end times and began to discover what I was being protected from. The revelations blew my mind.

If this entire system of eschatology is questionable, am I saying that Christ is not coming? Doesn't 2 Peter 3:3-4 tell us that "scoffers will come in the last days with scoffing… They will say, 'Where is the promise of his coming? For ever since the fathers fell asleep, all things are continuing as they were from the beginning of creation.'"

I'll address the theology of that passage in the appendix of this book, but for now suffice it to say that nothing I am about to explain questions the promise of Christ's coming. Rather, it questions certain *interpretations* of how that promised coming plays out. There is a difference between the Word of God and someone's *interpretation* of the Word of God. Interpretation is what I want to question, not God's Word.

And so it was that I began to question this dispensational eschatology of the end times. Though I considered other views to be wrong and still others to be heresy, I noticed that one view in particular delved into the time period directly after the book of Acts. It was the generation that led up to the destruction of Jerusalem and the holy temple in A.D. 70. In all my years of learning dispensational end times teaching, I never heard anything about this important time period in the life of Israel and the life of the church. It was like a black hole of historical knowledge. So out of my interest in history I studied it.

The scholars who explained this material stressed a way of interpreting the Bible that prioritized biblical context over our modern context. They explored the meaning of the bizarre symbols and images in the book of Revelation by finding their counterparts in the Old Testament, not in modern newspapers. It made sense to my evangelical focus on *sola scriptura*, the Bible as the first context of meaning and the final authority of doctrine. And that opened the door to a transformation of my understanding the Bible in its ancient Jewish and Near Eastern context.

Chapter 2
How Literalism Corrupts Bible Prophecy

The title of this chapter is a bit provocative. After all, isn't the Bible supposed to be taken literally? Isn't it only liberals and apostates who deny the literal truth of the Bible? When you interpret the Bible nonliterally, don't you end up believing it's just a bunch of religious myths? Well, no, actually. As a matter of fact, nobody takes the *entire* Bible literally. Not even those who say they do. Let me explain.

Nobody believes the hybrid sea beast of Revelation 13—with its ten horns on seven heads like a leopard, with a bear's feet and a lion's mouth—is a literal, biological, hybrid creature. Everyone believes it is figurative (at least everyone I've checked. I suppose there may be someone on the fringe who doesn't). We may not agree on what it symbolizes, but *everybody* believes it symbolizes something other than what it appears to be. Nobody thinks that in the last days this monster, or the land beast of Revelation 13:11, or the many hybrid creatures spoken of in Daniel's prophecies will roam the land as in a Godzilla movie. They are figurative symbols that represent evil kingdoms, as Daniel and the apostle John explained. Scripture says that God owns the cattle on a thousand hills (Psalm 50:10). Nobody believes that literally. Nobody believes that God does not own the cattle on the thousand-and-first hill or the two thousandth hill. Even literalists will admit that this is a figurative, poetic expression that God owns everything. Nobody believes that when Jesus said he was "the door" (John 10:7) that he was literally a wooden plank with hinges and a handle. This is a metaphor, a figure of speech that is not literally applicable, but operates as a symbol.

I could go on and on, and in this book I eventually will. But for now I just want to make the point that no right-thinking Christian believes that everything in the Bible is to be taken literally. It is a book full of figurative expression, poetry, hyperbole, symbol, allegory and metaphor. The question is not do we take the Bible literally, but *which parts* do we take literally and *which parts* do we take figuratively? The second question is the next obvious one: how do we know which parts are which? And that is not always an easy question to answer.

So when I say that literalism corrupts Bible prophecy, what I am really saying is that literalism taken to an extreme corrupts the interpretation of Bible prophecy by applying literalism where it was not intended by the biblical authors. I sometimes call this kind of excessive literalism "hyperliteralism." But again, no one, not even hyperliteralists, take everything in the Bible literally.

Selective Literalism

When I disagree with prophecy pundits, I often hear them retreat with the slogan, "Well, I take the Bible literally," as if they are the only ones who take the Bible seriously in its truth claims. But after I ask them a few questions, I find out that they in fact do not take everything in the Bible literally. *Because no one does. No one.* They'll believe that the battle of Gog and Magog in Ezekiel 38-39 talks of a literal war in our future. But, when pressed, they believe the bows, arrows, swords and chariots in the prophecy are not literal after all, but figurative or symbolic of modern armaments and vehicles. In other words, they do not take Ezekiel literally as they claim. Or, I will find out that they believe that Zechariah's prophecy of the plague that makes people's tongues rot in their mouths is a nuclear holocaust (Zech 14:12). They believe the description to be an ancient explanation of something modern that the ancient writers had no categories for understanding; so the prophets described it in terms they did understand. But it turns out that this interpretation is simply not literal. Nuclear blasts are not at all like plagues, and they don't make flesh rot; they burn it up like fire. So once again, "literalists" really don't believe everything in the text is literal. You could call this *selective literalism*, a literalism that is only literal when they want it to be and figurative when they don't want it to be. Of course everyone believes some things are literal and others are not. The problem is that those who claim to take the Bible literally often do not realize that they are just as figurative in many of their interpretations as anyone else. So again, the question is not whether Bible prophecy is to be interpreted literally or figuratively, but what parts are literal and what parts are figurative, and how do we know?

"You are just spiritualizing the text" is another slogan I have heard from literalists when they hear a symbolic interpretation of one of their favorite Bible prophecies. They may hear the claim that the new Jerusalem that comes from heaven in Revelation 21 is a poetic description of the spiritual meaning of the new covenant bride of Christ, the church, and they dismiss such interpretations as spiritualizing. But then those same people will say that the book of Revelation was not intended for the literal seven churches of Asia in the first century, as the text literally says, but for our modern generation thousands of years later. They, in fact, do spiritualize the text.

Everyone spiritualizes Scripture. *Everyone*. The problem is that we may disagree over which things should be spiritualized and which things should not. Spiritualizing is a common New Testament theological technique that the apostles used to interpret the new covenant. Jesus is the spiritualized Lamb of God—not a literal lamb with wool and hooves—who entered the spiritual sanctuary in heaven—not the literal one on earth (Heb 9:11-12). His literal death as a criminal on the cross was literally criminal punishment by earthly authorities and was spiritualized by God to be a sacrifice for our sins. The writer of Hebrews said that Jesus is right now crowned with glory and honor, with everything in subjection to his authority (Heb 2:8). But then he said that "we do not yet see everything in subjection to him," which spiritualizes that authority. It is real and true within the heavenly realm, but that truth is still in the process of being worked out in the physical world we live in. According to the Bible, much of what we see is not as things really are. Spiritualizing is simply a way of describing the spiritual reality that is not always seen behind the outer façade of history.

Think about it. Taking things spiritually can be just as literal as taking things literally. According to the New Testament, Jesus reigns in heaven right now at the right hand of God (Eph 1:20-21). But we don't see that throne in a physical sense. It is a spiritual reign in heaven. But is it any less literal? Of course not! Jesus literally reigns in heaven right now. It is not a figurative reign but a heavenly reign. So spiritual interpretations are not merely poetic or figurative references that are not real; they are literally true. It's just that they are not physically seen.

History and Symbolic Meaning

Does all this figurative language and spiritualizing mean that the resurrection of Jesus was figurative and not historical? Does this mean that God did not really part the Red Sea and that is only a made-up story symbolizing his spiritual deliverance? Of course not. Those who jump to this kind of conclusion are being guided by false either/or assumptions. Just because there is a lot of figurative language in the Bible does not mean that it is *all* figurative. The fact is that the Bible intertwines history with symbol and figurative language.

In my book When Giants Were Upon the Earth, I explained that Psalm 74 is a song describing the parting of the Red Sea.[1] Yet it gives that historical incident symbolic meaning by weaving in the notion that Yahweh "crushed the heads of Leviathan" (Psalm 74:13-14).

Leviathan in this passage is described as a single sea monster with multiple heads, like the mythical Hydra. In other passages we discover that Leviathan is a sea dragon of chaos (Isa 27:1; 51:9-10). The author of that Psalm wasn't telling a myth; he was investing an historical event with symbolic, spiritual significance. When God parted the Red Sea, it was like opening the door to establish his covenant with his people. Crushing the many heads of Leviathan was a spiritualized poetic expression of Yahweh conquering chaos to establish his order and his power over those forces of chaos.

When the historical writer of the book of Judges told the story of Sisera and his battle with Israel at the Kishon river, he likened the battling kings to stars in heaven.

> Judges 5:19–20
>
> The kings came, they fought; then fought the kings of Canaan…
>
> From heaven the stars fought, from their courses they fought against Sisera.

---

[1] Brian Godawa, *When Giants Were Upon the Earth: The Watchers, The Nephilim, and the Cosmic War of the Seed* (Los Angeles, Embedded Pictures Publishing, 2014), 79-88.

This interweaving of history and poetry (spiritualizing) is not exclusive to the ancient Hebrews. We do it today, don't we? We call celebrities "stars" and talk about how sports teams "destroy" each other in their games. We say things like, "9-11 turned the world upside down," and other such symbolic statements. As New Testament scholar N.T. Wright explained,

> We do this all the time ourselves. I have often pointed out to students that to describe the fall of the Berlin Wall, as one well might, as an "earth-shattering event" might perhaps lead some future historian, writing in the *Martian Journal of Early European Studies* to hypothesize that an earthquake caused the collapse of the Wall, leading to both sides realizing they could live together after all. A good many of apocalyptic literature in our own century operate on about that level of misunderstanding.[2]

Everyone weaves symbolism and figurative language into literal history. This happens in prophecy even more so. The issue is how do we know what is literal and what is figurative, what is physical and what is spiritual? Is there a standard that we can use to avoid the chaos of infinite interpretations based on someone's personal whims and fancies?

Cheer up! That foreboding sea is about to part.

The Plain Sense of Scripture

When I first studied the Bible, I was taught that Bible believers interpret the Bible literally. This means that atheists and liberals who don't believe the Bible is God's Word don't believe it is historically or factually true. They don't interpret the Bible literally. They tend to reduce it to myths and fables made up by religious leaders in order to control the people. In contrast, if you are a Christian, you are supposed to believe the Bible is literally true. So "literal" usually means historical or factual in this view, that it's not a myth or a made-up fairy tale. This isn't really a good definition of literal, but it is the connotation our culture assumes. So we're stuck with it for now.

---

[2]N. T. Wright, *The New Testament and the People of God* (Minneapolis: Fortress, 1992), p. 282.

In my book The Imagination of God I make the case, instead, for taking the Bible *literarily*, meaning as the literary text was intended.[3] Sometimes a piece of literature is intended to be factual or historical, sometimes poetic or figurative, oftentimes both. So it is the literary context that determines how a scripture should be understood, not our expectations that we bring to the text. Since the Bible is literature with different genres and styles of writing, we should be *literary* in our interpretation, not literal.

But in my earlier days, I didn't have that finer distinction. And as I dug deeper into Bible prophecy in particular, I discovered that the dispensational viewpoint did in fact have some awareness of the poetry or figurative language in the Bible. How could it not? But because of its bias of literal interpretation as a priority over figurative interpretation, this view forged a standard of Bible hermeneutics that favored that bias. One of the more popular expressions of the standard of literal interpretation of the Bible is embodied in an often-quoted paragraph by David Cooper.

> When the plain sense of Scripture makes common sense, seek no other sense; therefore, take every word at its primary, ordinary, usual, literal meaning unless the facts of the immediate context, studied in the light of related passages and axiomatic and fundamental truths, indicate clearly otherwise.[4]

That made perfect sense to my Bible-believing reason. In order to avoid the anarchy and relativism of every man's interpretation being right in his own eyes, we must take the Bible at face value. We must use our common sense to understand the plain sense of Scripture. We can't just go turning anything we like, willy nilly, into esoteric symbols and arcane allegories. Ordinary and usual seemed superior to extraordinary and unusual. I agreed—and I still agree today—that words should not be taken out of context. They should be understood within their immediate context as well as the context

---

[3] Brian Godawa, *The Imagination of God: Art, Creativity and Truth in the Bible* (Los Angeles, Embedded Pictures Publishing, 2016), 13-35.
[4] David L. Cooper, *The World's Greatest Library: Graphically Illustrated* (Los Angeles: Biblical Research Society, 1970), 11.

of other Scripture. That remains a sound hermeneutic rule of interpretation: first and foremost, let Scripture interpret Scripture.

There was only one problem that I was about to discover: *my* plain and common sense, *my* ordinary and usual understanding is not at all the same as *the ancient Hebrew* plain and common sense, or ordinary and usual understanding. It wasn't until I began to study the ancient Hebrew mindset, steeped as it was in the Old Testament and influenced by a Near Eastern mindset, that I began to realize just how different that was from my mindset, steeped as it is in a modern American, Western worldview and in scientific categories of thinking.

Language Determines Meaning

Consider this: we are modern Westerners reading an English translation of the Bible that was written in different languages (Hebrew, Greek, Aramaic). Every language has its own colloquialisms and structures of knowledge. Language embodies a worldview that does not often translate through the words. How often do we have trouble understanding what a modern German or French or Arabic phrase means because we don't have an equivalent in our own culture? Mere translation of words and even phrases is not enough. Humor differs from language to language, culture to culture. So does poetry. For example, accurately translating the Hebrew phrase into English, "You [Yahweh] crushed the heads of Leviathan" (Ps 74:13–14), does not convey to us what would have been obvious to the ancient Hebrew. We might be tempted to think that the author is writing about real giant sea creatures. But the ancient Hebrew would immediately understand the poetic expression of God overcoming chaos (the sea dragon) by establishing his covenant order. Order out of chaos.

Also, many Bible readers don't realize that there are many words, phrases, and grammar in their English Bibles that are only guesses of the correct translation. Readers may not know this because the translators have to commit to something or they couldn't publish their work. So the English reader reads the text and doesn't see all the ambiguity and questioning behind the choice of words. The English Standard Version of the Bible translates Isaiah 34:14, a passage describing the destruction of the nation of Edom, as "Indeed, there the night bird settles and finds for herself a resting place." But the word for "night bird" is *lilith*, a word with unknown meaning. The translators settle on "night bird," but the truth is that Lilith may be a reference to a pagan deity of that name. A passage that the ancient Hebrew would understand as aggressive mockery of paganism is translated in English into a mere passive colorless description.

And even if the translated Bible words are correct, there is often sufficient ambiguity in the meaning of the language to support conflicting interpretations. Take, for instance, the phrase "the sign of the Son of Man" in Matthew 24:30. The English Standard Version and others read, "Then will appear in heaven the sign of the Son of Man." But the New International Version, and others read, "Then will appear the sign of the Son of Man in heaven." According to Bible commentators and expositors, the grammar of this sentence could either mean that there will be a sign in the sky of the Son of Man, or that the Son of Man will appear in the sky as a sign, or that there will be a sign that appears somewhere that shows that the Son of Man is enthroned in heaven, not the sky. I will explore these possibilities later. But for now I just want to make the point that translations are complicated and so are languages and cultures. The plain sense of an English translation is not the plain sense of the original Greek or Hebrew Bible. So when someone uses that phrase, "plain sense" of the Bible, they often do not realize how unbiblical their plain sense really is.

On a smaller scale, imagine a modern Millennial reading something from the 1980s. Some slang and lingo would be almost gibberish to that reader. The word "bad" actually meant "good." "Dexter" was not a TV serial killer, but a word meaning "nerdy." "Down" meant "up." A "Stella" was a "preppy," and on and on. Okay, it's not as if the meanings would be totally alien, but the point is that if language and culture can change so much within a culture over a few decades, imagine how much more truly alien an outside culture would be from ours that is a few thousand years and half a world removed from us. Even when we translate the words correctly, we don't necessarily translate the cultural meaning. In translation alone our plain sense is not necessarily their plain sense.

The Genre of Prophecy and Apocalyptic

But more important than translation is the genre of a piece of literature. You can get the translation right, but if you don't understand the genre you will get it completely wrong. Such is the nature of the genres of apocalypse, prophecy and dream visions. They are decidedly symbolic. The apostle John writes in the Greek of the very first verse of Revelation 1:1 that the angel "sent and signified" the Revelation to John. The images in Revelation are signs or symbols for something else. If the reader takes them literally or in their "plain sense," they will misinterpret the text. Literal isn't everything when it comes to genre.

Different genres of writing have different purposes and therefore should be interpreted through different lenses than the ordinary and usual. The genre of ancient Hebrew prophecy and apocalypse in the Bible is anything but ordinary and usual. It is actually extraordinary and unusual. It is certainly not driven by the notion of plain sense or literal meaning. It is a highly poetic genre expressed in visions and dreams of fantastic images and poetry of symbolism and metaphor.

In the next chapters we are going to take a look at specific examples of the poetry, symbolism, and metaphors of Bible prophecy in order to discern the difference between the literal and the figurative. The goal of this chapter has been to deconstruct the very popular approach to literalism (or hyperliteralism, if you will) in Bible prophecy. It just doesn't hold up as a consistent interpretive approach. We must learn how to exegete the poetry of prophecy as an art, not a science. And art is tricky, ambiguous, and unclear at times. It evades our control.

And prophecy does not exist in a vacuum of our modern understanding. The Jewish writers of Scripture used repetitious images, motifs, and patterns of writing that have precedents in Scripture itself. Rather than interpreting the ancient prophecies through *our* eyes, we must seek to interpret it through *their* eyes and worldview. Before we try to envision the locusts with human heads and scorpion tails as modern Cobra helicopters, we should first see how locusts and human traits on animals and scorpions were used in the Old Testament, since that was the world within which they lived and breathed and had their very being.

It turns out that the commonly used standard we cited above of interpreting the Bible through our plain sense, common sense, ordinary and usual meaning is an act of cultural prejudice. Our Western plain sense literalism is simply not the priority in a very symbolic genre of a different culture with a different plain sense than ours, different colloquialisms and memes than ours, and a different sense of what is ordinary and usual.

It turns out that interpreting Bible prophecy with our modern, Western, hyperliteralistic plain sense will almost certainly result in a false interpretation of the text. If anything, the principle for interpreting poetic symbolic literature like Bible prophecy should be the opposite of the plain sense approach. So I herewith propose a rewrite of the hermeneutic principle applied to prophecy.

> When the plain sense of prophecy makes sense, beware your own bias and seek the genre sense. Take every word at its primary, extraordinary, symbolic meaning unless the facts of the immediate context, studied in the light of related passages and historical facts, indicate clearly otherwise.

PART TWO
The Poetry of Old Testament Prophecy

Chapter 3
The Day of the Lord

Prophecy is not a science. It is an art of poetry and symbolism. So much interpretation of Bible prophecy today is made through the perspective of a modern reader that often fails to take into account the ancient Hebrew context and usage of prophecy. If you read a prophecy and want to understand what the writer intended, wouldn't it be wise to consult the rest of the Bible to see if that word, image or phrase is used elsewhere, and, if so, what it meant to him?

Sadly, this is not the practice of many prophecy pundits today who read some fantastic imagery and automatically assume that the passage simply must be referring to the future (futurism) because it could not possibly have occurred in the past (preterism).

What follows will be some crucial examples of prophetic concepts and phrases that I think are too often misunderstood through our modern bias. I want to reaffirm that my goal in these next couple chapters is not to defend a particular eschatology of the end times. Of course I do have a specific view of the end times, but I want to find common ground first, not pick a fight. None of what I say here is owned by a single eschatology. You can be a dispensationalist, premillennialist, amillennialist, or postmillennialist and you should be able to agree with what I am about to explain. My hope is that we will all prioritize the Bible over our own bias and let Scripture interpret Scripture before we start applying anything to our own time period.

Those concerned with end times Bible prophecy often refer to the *day of the Lord*, a phrase used many times by Old Testament prophets. It refers to God's judgment and sounds pretty universal, final and absolute, end of the world stuff, doesn't it? On the surface it would seem to match up with the second coming of Christ and the final judgment of the living and the dead. Some Bible teachers will rattle off different passages from the Old Testament to prove that God has prophesied this future, single day of the

Lord over and over in different contexts. Here are some of them. The underlining is mine.

> Zephaniah 1:14–18
> The great day of the LORD is near, near and hastening fast... [15] A day of wrath is that day, a day of distress and anguish, a day of ruin and devastation, a day of darkness and gloom, a day of clouds and thick darkness... [18] on the day of the wrath of the LORD. In the fire of his jealousy, all the earth shall be consumed; for a full and sudden end he will make of all the inhabitants of the earth.

> Joel 2:1–11
> Blow a trumpet in Zion; sound an alarm on my holy mountain! Let all the inhabitants of the land tremble, for the day of the LORD is coming; it is near, [2] a day of darkness and gloom, a day of clouds and thick darkness!... [10] The earth quakes before them; the heavens tremble. The sun and the moon are darkened, and the stars withdraw their shining. [11]...For the day of the LORD is great and very awesome; who can endure it?

> Isaiah 13:6–11
> Wail, for the day of the LORD is near; as destruction from the Almighty it will come... [9] Behold, the day of the LORD comes, cruel, with wrath and fierce anger, to make the land a desolation and to destroy its sinners from it. [10] For the stars of the heavens and their constellations will not give their light; the sun will be dark at its rising, and the moon will not shed its light. [11] I will punish the world for its evil, and the wicked for their iniquity.

In these passages above, we read about the day of the Lord coming in terms that must surely have to do with the end of the world since they are cataclysmic and worldwide: "all the earth shall be consumed," "all the inhabitants of the earth," "the sun, moon, and stars darkened," God "punishing the world." In other passages, like Isaiah 34, we read about how the "host of heaven shall be dissolved" and "the sky rolled up like a scroll" on the Lord's "day of vengeance." Jeremiah said that the "day of vengeance" would constitute God "avenging himself upon his foes."

Futurists feel assured that these prophecies are warnings of the final judgment at the end of history. There's only one problem—they're not. Don't get me wrong. I am not denying a future final judgment. I do believe in a final judgment, but these passages are not referring to that day. The day of the Lord in the prophets is not a single day at the end of history. "Day of the Lord" is a colloquial phrase that refers to *any time* that God judges a city, a people or a nation. The day of the Lord is not a generic term of universal judgment, but a specific term of localized judgment. I'll prove it to you.

I will address the apparent universal terminology of "all the earth" and "sun, moon, and stars" later. For now, the key to interpreting the fulfillment of the day of the Lord is in the text. God himself told us how these prophecies were already fulfilled in history, not our modern future. The prophecy of Zephaniah 1 was made sometime before 621 B.C., the time of King Josiah's reform in Israel. Zephaniah gave his oracle of judgment against Judah and Jerusalem of that day because they were corrupted with idol worship (1:4, 10-13). Then he predicted the fall of Nineveh (2:13-16) that occurred in 612 B.C. and condemned other peoples that surrounded Judah at the time, like Moab, Ammon, and Philistine cities.[1] The day of the Lord in Zephaniah described God's *local* judgment of ancient Judah, as well as Israel's enemies *of that time period.* The apparently universal language of "utterly sweeping away everything from the face of the earth," are spiritualized hyperbole, exaggerated expressions of the spiritual reality.

Joel's words in Joel 2 were made against the city of Jerusalem besieged by Mesopotamian forces before being taken into exile. The book is not easily placed historically, but commentator Douglas Stuart concluded, "The words of the book would likely have been spoken on one of these occasions: the Assyrian invasion of 701 B.C., the Babylonian invasion of 598, or the Babylonian invasion of 588."[2] The invasion and exile of Israel in the 7th or

---

[1] Ralph L. Smith, *Micah–Malachi, vol. 32,* Word Biblical Commentary (Dallas: Word, Incorporated, 1998), 122.

[2] Douglas Stuart, *Hosea–Jonah, vol. 31*, Word Biblical Commentary (Dallas: Word, Incorporated, 2002), 226.

8th centuries B.C. was the day of the Lord in Joel, not a future end of the world. The events of the sun and the moon being darkened, and the stars withdrawing their shining occurred during the invasion of the foreign godless nation. What did that look like? We'll look more closely in the next chapters.

The day of the Lord in Isaiah 13 above was explicitly stated as being the localized judgment against Babylon when it fell to the Medes in 539 B.C. (13:1, 17-19). The Lord's day of vengeance in Isaiah 34 was against Edom in the 8th century B.C. (34:5, 6, 9). The Lord's day of vengeance in Jeremiah 46 was a description of the fall of Egypt to Babylon's Nebuchadnezzar during the time of Judah's King Jehoiakim (46:2). Isaiah 34 and Jeremiah 46 were fulfilled in past history. Now re-read those prophecies as fulfilled and you can see how the universal language is clearly the spiritual reality behind localized judgments on cities and nations.

But that's not all. Amos described Israel's northern kingdom destruction by the Assyrians around 722 B.C. as the day of the Lord (Amos 5:18-20), and Obadiah's day of the Lord for Edom and other nations was sometime after the fall of Jerusalem to Babylon in 586 B.C.[3]

This survey of the passages that use the phrase "day of the Lord" shows that it is not a reference to a single event of universal judgment in our modern day future, but a term used of multiple events of local judgments already fulfilled in history. When God judged individual cities, peoples, or nations in the Old Testament, it would be their "day of the Lord," their historical comeuppance, or retribution. So when prophecy teachers quote all these Old Testament passages to draw out what they think will happen in our future, they are quoting Bible verses out of context and applying them to events the original writers did not intend and the text does not justify. When modern teachers say that these prophecies have a double fulfillment—meaning that they also apply to an end of the world final judgment—they are arbitrarily imposing their preconceived desires on the text. You could certainly say that by analogy the final judgment will be another day of the

[3] John H Walton, Zondervan Illustrated Bible Backgrounds Commentary (Old Testament): *The Minor Prophets, Job, Psalms, Proverbs, Ecclesiastes, Song of Songs, vol. 5* (Grand Rapids, MI: Zondervan, 2009), 93.

Lord for all peoples in history, but you could not say that these Old Testament passages are prophesying specifically about that day.

The End Was Near

Another aspect of these Old Testament days of the Lord that highlights their historical fulfillment is the explicit timing. Zephaniah repeated the word "near" several times to emphasize the point that the day of the Lord's judgment would happen soon. "The great day of the LORD is near, near and hastening fast" (1:14). Zephaniah didn't say it was far, far in the future, thousands of years away. Actually it was so near that it happened to that original Jewish audience.

Joel repeated himself as well when writing, "The day of the LORD is near" (1:15), "the day of the LORD is coming: it is near" (2:1), and then a third time in 3:14. And what do you know? It *was* near—to those Jews who were punished by God with exile, not some future generation thousands of years later.

Isaiah said, "The day of the LORD is near" (13:6). And, sure enough, it was near because within a few near years the Medes actually did overthrow Babylon like Sodom and Gomorrah, just as Isaiah said they would (13:17-19). "Near" really meant near to the audience, not far in the future.

Obadiah's day of the Lord was near (v. 15) for the Philistines, Samaria, the Edomites, and all "the Canaanites as far as Zarephath" (v. 18-21) because the Babylonians plundered all of the land of Israel with its inhabitants in the 8th century B.C.—not in the 21st century A.D.

Amos described the day of the Lord for Israel in the Assyrian conquest of Israel of 722 B.C. in near terms as well. "The end has come upon my people Israel" (8:2). The conclusion is inescapable; when the prophets said the day of the Lord was near for these nations, it really was near, usually within their lifetimes.

The obvious objection is raised that if prophecy is so poetic, why can't the time reference be poetic? After all, "with the Lord one day is as a thousand years, and a thousand years as one day" (2 Pet 3:8). Remember, history and poetry is interwoven, so we must discern where those differences are. And it seems evident that if the term "day of the Lord" is described as judgment on certain cities and peoples and then we see that those events did in fact occur historically near to the time the prophecies were given, doesn't that tell you that "near" is probably not a poetic reference to the far future but actually means what it says? You would have to deny the clear facts and replace them with a conspiracy theory of alternate predictions.

In these Old Testament prophesies, "near" really means historically near, not poetically distant.

What then do we make of it when the term "day of the Lord" is used in the New Testament? Surely that would be a reference to the final judgment at the end of history? We will take a look at that later when I walk through Jesus' Olivet Discourse on the topic. For now, I just want to establish that the day of the Lord in the Old Testament was not a reference to a single, worldwide judgment of mankind at the end of history, but a poetic expression that was used of many different localized judgments of cities, peoples, and nations throughout history.

At this point some may object and say that despite the references to localized historical judgments in prophecies about the day of the Lord, there must be some kind of double fulfillment in a future referent because of other elements of those prophecies that are clearly universal and therefore could not have happened yet. Phrases like "all the nations," "sun, moon, and stars," as well as astronomic or global catastrophes like the sky rolling up like a scroll indicate that these days of the Lord could not have happened yet. Therefore, they must be universal and global instead of singular and local, distant in the future and not "near" to the prophet's time in history.

It is to those terms that we now turn.

Chapter 4
All the Nations

There are other phrases used in conjunction with the Old Testament day of the Lord that used to make me sure it was speaking of a singularity in my future and not just something fulfilled in Israel's past. That was the universal and global language of judgment on "all the nations" or "all the earth." I thought that surely God had not judged all the nations yet and surely the language of the whole earth was not fulfilled in the days of ancient Israel.

I was wrong. As I studied the issue more closely, I began to see how much holy hyperbole God used in his Word. At first this was unsettling. I mean, isn't exaggeration a form of deception? Wouldn't that make God wrong, or worse, a liar? Wouldn't God speak precisely when he was communicating his truth? Or was I placing an inappropriate demand on the Bible? If I accepted Scripture on its own terms instead of mine, then shouldn't I first find out what it says and then adjust my theology to fit that truth, rather than define how I think God should communicate and then force that prejudice on the Bible to make it fit? I soon began to learn my own demands were quite unreasonable and illiterate. God used hyperbole, tons and tons of it!

Does "All" Always Mean All?

The first step I had to take before I could understand the concept of "all the nations," was to understand the underlying concept of the Jewish nation as a "chosen people," in contrast with the Gentiles around them. Here is what I discovered.

One of the most prominent memes in the Old Testament is that of Israel versus the Gentiles, or the nations. From the time of the Tower of Babel onward, God had decided to choose a single nation out of all the nations to be his people. That nation would be Israel, the descendants of Jacob.

> Deuteronomy 32:8–9
> When the Most High gave to the nations their inheritance, when he divided mankind, he fixed the borders of the peoples according to the number of the sons of God. [9] But the LORD's portion is his people, Jacob his allotted heritage.

God's nation did not begin to appear on the scene until its forefather Abraham, but God sovereignly determined that the world would be separated into two bodies of people, his people and the Gentiles. The Greek word for "Gentiles" is *ethnos* which means "nations" or "people." It's where we get our word *ethnic*. So it is no surprise that the Scriptures are full of generic references to the nations, meaning "everyone who isn't part of God's people." This bred an "us versus them" mentality among the Jews, even to the point that during Jesus' day, the word "sinner" was a synonym for Gentile. You were either a saved Jew or you were a lost sinner Gentile.

So when God said in Joel's prophecy concerning the day of the Lord that he would gather "all the nations" and enter into judgment with them (Joel 3:2), he was not using the term in our modern sense of every nation on the spherical globe. He qualified this term of "all the nations" later when he explained his judgment on "all the surrounding nations" in the land of Israel at that time (3:11, 12), specifically Tyre, Sidon, and the regions of Philistia (3:4). "All the nations" did not mean every nation on the face of the globe, including those in the Americas. It simply meant all those nations at that time who were in Israel's local area of influence. "All the nations" is a generic reference that can refer to a select group of Gentile people in contrast with God's people. In Joel "all the nations" meant Tyre, Sidon, and the regions of Philistia.

When Jeremiah prophesied against "all the nations" (Jer 25:13), he also didn't mean all the nations on the face of the globe; he meant "many nations" (25:14), specifically those he was sent to (25:17). When Zechariah wrote that "all the nations of the earth will gather against" Judah and Jerusalem (Zech 12:3), he didn't mean all nations on the face of the globe including those in the Americas; he meant those surrounding peoples who were not God's people and who would besiege Jerusalem. So we see that the phrase "all the nations" is a synonym for any group of people who are not God's people, not every nation on the face of the globe. It's hyperbole with an ethnic twist.

A popular phrase in some Bible circles is "All means all and that's all it means." They think they are simply reading the plain sense of the Bible, but in fact they are importing their own meaning onto the text. The truth is that in the Bible, "all" does not always mean all. Here are some other passages that illustrate that "all nations" does not mean literally all nations but is a poetic reference to many nations, or some nations that are not God's people.

In Jeremiah 28, King Nebuchadnezzar of Babylon is referred to as king with a yoke over the necks of "all the nations" (28:11). But Nebuchadnezzar was not king over all the nations outside of Babylon. It was common to use the hyperbole of "all the nations" to express the power of a king over everyone *in their local sphere of existence*, in this case, the empire of Babylon.

All does not always mean all.

In 1 Chronicles 14:17, David's fame is described as going out "into all the lands; and the LORD brought the fear of him on all the nations." It would be ludicrous to suggest that this text means that the fear of David was on the lands of the Americas and others outside of the immediate vicinity of Israel at that time. It is hyperbole that means widespread influence.

In the Bible, *all nations* simply does not always mean every nation that exists.

On the day of Pentecost in Acts 2:5 we read that there were Jews in Jerusalem "from every nation under heaven." The nations listed (2:5-11) are close to the original seventy nations of Genesis 10, but not precisely. And they do not include any nations from the other side of the globe. Why? Because the hyperbolic phrase "every nation under heaven" does not literally mean every nation under heaven. It is poetic hyperbole. It is a theological message that God is undoing the Babel separation of nations with the kingdom of God. He would unify the separated nations of the earth by having the same gospel spoken in the separate tongues of those original seventy nations. But it is not a mathematically precise one-to-one correspondence of those seventy nations, and it is not literally every single nation under heaven because it does not include those on the other side of the globe. This is not an imperfection in the biblical text. It is not a contradiction or historical inaccuracy. It is poetic writing. It was never intended to be scientifically precise. It is theological hyperbole. "All the nations" is a poetic phrase that is used to mean *many* or even *some* Gentile peoples. So when God speaks about judging all the nations, it is not necessarily a reference to the universal final judgment at the end of time, but rather a localized judgment against some specific people as a representative of non-Israelite nations.

All does not always mean all, and that's not all it means.

But what about the massive astronomical and geological catastrophes spoken of in so many prophecies? Certainly those indicate the universe as we know it at the end of the world. Let's take a closer look at that collapsing universe imagery in the next chapter.

Chapter 5
Cosmic Catastrophes

When I was a hyperliteralist I thought that in order to maintain the integrity and inspiration of the Bible, I had to interpret the descriptions of God's judgments literally or else I might slip into liberal theology and end up renouncing the faith. I thought that when God said something, he meant it. And if he said he was going to roll the sky up like a scroll, then, by golly, he would literally roll up that sky like a scroll. After all, he parted the Red Sea and raised people from the dead, didn't he? He created the universe by merely speaking it forth, and so destroying it with the kind of monumental damage described in prophecies would certainly not be all that more miraculous in comparison. Maybe rolling up the sky would be another way of saying he created a wormhole. God can do anything, so I should believe him when he said he would roll up the sky like a scroll. And once again I assumed these prophecies spoke about the final judgment because they had "obviously" not happened yet.

What I eventually came to realize was that God didn't mean he would literally or scientifically roll up the sky like a scroll. He wasn't hiding modern quantum physics in ancient texts. That was my biased, modern, scientific mind imposing itself over the text. God was actually using creative poetic language to describe the spiritual reality behind what he was doing in history.

Covenant as Creation

It all began with learning to appreciate the creation language in the Bible as a means of communicating the value of his covenant with his people. When God created the heavens and the earth in Genesis 1, he was creating order out of the chaos of Genesis 1:2, the formlessness and emptiness of creation. Part of that created order was the sun, moon, and stars. They were to separate light and dark and be for signs and seasons

(1:14-15). In ancient Near Eastern religions, people pictured the gods fighting the sea (a symbol of chaos) as an expression of their rule and power to illustrate their creation of order out of chaos. The Hebrew scriptures do the same thing, only in a way that says Yahweh is the true God. He is the one who created his covenant order within the chaos of the world.[1]

Psalm 74 is a good example of this creation and covenant motif out of the chaos of the sea. Read this passage and notice how God had power over the chaos of the sea when he established his covenant through Moses. But then read on and you will see the language of creation connected to that covenant.

> Psalm 74:13–17
> You divided the sea by your might; you broke the heads of the sea monsters on the waters. [14] You crushed the heads of Leviathan; you gave him as food for the creatures of the wilderness. [15] You split open springs and brooks; you dried up ever-flowing streams. [16] Yours is the day, yours also the night; you have established the heavenly lights and the sun. [17] You have fixed all the boundaries of the earth.

The creation language of the sun, moon, and stars separating day and night is part of God fixing or establishing the boundaries of the earth. God's covenant with Israel is described in the language of creation of the universe. It is poetic metaphor, an image that stands for something else.

Isaiah also wrote about the Mosaic covenant beginning when God conquered the chaos of the Red Sea. Creating God's people, Zion, is expressed in terms of Genesis 1, establishing the heavens and earth.

> Isaiah 51:15–16
> I am the LORD your God, who stirs up the sea so that its waves roar— the LORD of hosts is his name. [16] And I have put my words in your mouth and covered you in the shadow of my hand, establishing the heavens and laying the

---

[1] For a detailed description of this motif of creation out of chaos in the ancient world, see the chapter "Leviathan," in my book *When Giants Were Upon the Earth* (California, Embedded Pictures Publishing, 2014), 79-88..

> foundations of the earth, and saying to Zion, "You are my people."

So we see that God described his covenantal relationship in the cosmic terms of creation, including the sun, moon, and stars. He created order out of chaos with his covenantal rule. Creating his covenantal order with his people was spiritually likened to the creation of the heavens and the earth.

It makes perfect sense then that when his covenantal relationship was violated, it would be described in the terms of the destruction of creation. Theologians call this "decreation."

When God destroyed the holy temple, the symbol of God's covenant, in 587 B.C. through the Babylonians, he used the cosmic terms of all of creation being undone. It's told in the terms of a reversal of Genesis 1.

> Jeremiah 4:23–28
> I looked on the earth, and behold, it was without form and void; and to the heavens, and they had no light. [24] I looked on the mountains, and behold, they were quaking, and all the hills moved to and fro. [25] I looked, and behold, there was no man, and all the birds of the air had fled. [26] I looked, and behold, the fruitful land was a desert, and all its cities were laid in ruins before the LORD, before his fierce anger. [27] For thus says the LORD, "The whole land shall be a desolation; yet I will not make a full end. [28] For this the earth shall mourn, and the heavens above be dark; for I have spoken."

These cosmic disturbances did not occur literally when this prophecy was fulfilled. The earth did not return to the original state of chaos, "without form and void"; men and birds did not vanish from the earth; the sun, moon, and stars did not literally go dark. These were all decreation terms to express the spiritual reality of God's covenantal relationship being violated.

Sun, Moon, and Stars

God used these same terms of a collapsing universe to describe the destruction of Babylon by the Medes in 539 B.C. If a nation's covenant order is like the "heavens and the earth," their destruction is like the destruction of the heavens and the earth.

> Isaiah 13:9–11
> Behold, the day of the LORD comes, cruel, with wrath and fierce anger, to make the land a desolation and to destroy its sinners from it. [10] For the stars of the heavens and their constellations will not give their light; the sun will be dark at its rising, and the moon will not shed its light. [11] I will punish the world for its evil, and the wicked for their iniquity.

These cosmic catastrophes were not literal. When the Medes overran Babylon as this prophecy predicted, the sun, moon, and stars did not go dark. If the sun went dark, the entire solar system would have been destroyed. Sun, moon, and stars are not merely creation metaphors, they are also symbols of the spiritual power and authority behind earthly rulers. The ancient Hebrews, like their Near Eastern neighbors, believed that behind the earthly power of human rulers was the power of the heavenly beings that they likened to stars in the heavens, calling them the heavenly host. So when a nation's rulers lost power that was described as if the sun, moon, and stars lost their light or their power.[2]

When God said in Isaiah 34:4 that "all the host of heaven shall rot away, and the skies roll up like a scroll. All their host shall fall, as leaves fall from the vine, like leaves falling from the fig tree," he was poetically describing the fall of Edom's spiritual and earthly power in the light of God's judgment (34:5). He was not describing literal stars falling to earth. They would burn up the earth long before they got within the earth's orbit. Meteors are not stars, so you couldn't interpret that literally even if you wanted to. And the sky did not roll away in some kind of reverse gravity stargate wormhole in 587 B.C. when this prophecy was fulfilled.

When Egypt was destroyed by Babylon around 580 B.C., the prophet Ezekiel prophesied that event with the following description: "I will cover the heavens and make their stars dark; I will cover the sun with a cloud and the moon will not give its light. All the bright lights of heaven will I make

---

[2] On heavenly powers behind earthly powers, see Brian Godawa, *When Giants Were Upon the Earth: The Watchers, The Nephilim, and the Cosmic War of the Seed* (Los Angeles, Embedded Pictures Publishing, 2014), 278-284.

dark over you and put darkness on your land" (Ezek 32:7-8, 11). You could say that dark clouds could achieve a certain amount of this effect, but certainly not all of it. The darkening of the heavenly host was a common metaphor for powers losing their authority.

When Israel was destroyed and led into captivity by Nebuchadnezzar in the 6th century B.C., Isaiah used the same poetic metaphor of sun, moon, and stars as symbols of spiritual powers linked to earthly powers.

> Isaiah 24:21–23
> On that day the LORD will punish the host of heaven, in heaven, and the kings of the earth, on the earth. [22] They will be gathered together as prisoners in a pit; they will be shut up in a prison, and after many days they will be punished. [23] Then the moon will be confounded and the sun ashamed.

In the Bible cosmic catastrophe or collapsing universe imagery, including the sun, moon, and stars losing their light, is a poetic device for figuratively describing the fall of earthly rulers and the spiritual powers behind them, not literal astronomical phenomena and not a literal end to the space-time universe. As N.T. Wright has explained, this view remained even into the first century time of the New Testament.

> Within the mainline Jewish writings of this period, covering a wide range of styles, genres, political persuasions and theological perspectives, *there is virtually no evidence that Jews were expecting the end of the space-time universe.* There is abundant evidence that they, like Jeremiah and others before them, knew a good metaphor when they saw one, and used cosmic imagery to bring out the full theological significance of cataclysmic socio-political events. There is almost nothing to suggest that they followed the Stoics into the belief that the world itself would come to an end; and there is almost everything—their stories, their symbols, their praxis, not least their tendency to revolution, and their entire theology—to suggest that they did not.

> What, then, did they believe was going to happen? They believed that *the present world order* would come to an end—the world order in which pagans held power, and Jews, the covenant people of the creator god, did not.[3]

Concluding Remarks

This brief examination of Old Testament prophecies should illustrate that all the extreme language of cosmic proportions that are used to describe God's judgment in Scripture—such as the day of the Lord, all the nations, and sun, moon, and stars falling into darkness—does not refer to literal, physical events for a universal end of the world and final judgment. They are poetic descriptions of local judgments of cities, peoples, and nations in history. And God used "heaven and earth" creation and destruction language to express how spiritually important those events were. The prophetic language of cosmic catastrophe is about the *spiritual importance* of what was to happen, not a *physical description* of what was to happen.

This is only the tip of the ziggurat of metaphors, analogies, similes, and other poetic devices that God used to describe spiritual reality in the Old Testament. But what about the same fantastic imagery that shows up in the New Testament? Is that about a final judgment, or could it be about a local judgment as well? Are modern prophecy pundits correct to claim that we are about to experience geological upheavals and astronomical catastrophes in our near future?

I think you can already see the answer coming. But let's not jump to conclusions. In order to answer that question, we need to take a closer look at the poetry of New Testament prophecy.

---

[3] N. T. Wright, *The New Testament and the People of God*, Christian Origins and the Question of God (London: Society for Promoting Christian Knowledge, 1992), 333.

PART THREE
The Poetry of New Testament Prophecy

Chapter 6
The Olivet Discourse

When I first began to take a closer look at the end times, I was a hyperliteralist and a dispensationalist. I believed the standard Hal Lindsey or *Left Behind* scenario. The nation state of Israel was God's people about whom most of the end times prophecies were made. I thought it was clear from the New Testament that we were living in the last days and that the signs were all around us. I thought that within my generation the Christians would be raptured and things would get worse in the world until a false world savior arose, promising to rescue us all. He would be the Antichrist, who would then make a pact with Israel and rebuild the temple. Seven years of great tribulation would begin with the persecution of those "left behind" who turned to God. After three-and-a-half years, that Antichrist would set up a statue of himself in the temple in Jerusalem, make that "Beast" come to life, and force everyone to receive the mark of the Beast. During this time, Jews would realize their rejection of Jesus as the Messiah and repent *en masse*. The Antichrist would persecute those believing Jews and gather all the nations as allies in order to invade Israel in the battle of Armageddon. Jesus would then return to destroy the Antichrist and all his minions, save Jerusalem and the remnant of those Jews, and set up a thousand-year reign on earth at Jerusalem called the millennium. From that city he would reinstitute the temple sacrifices as a memorial and rule until Satan would make one last attack on Jesus and his followers. But Satan and his minions would lose and be thrown into the lake of fire. This would be followed by the resurrection of the dead and the final judgment.

I thought this was the clear picture predicted in Scripture. Sure, there were minor differences, like when the rapture would happen—pretribulation, midtribulation, or posttribulation. But this entire premillennial scenario seemed to echo through all Scripture and especially through the book of Revelation.

Until I studied other viewpoints.

Then I began a journey of many years toward a new position. But it was not easy. As I have already admitted, I initially reacted against other views with hostility and insult. It would take years before I could see the big picture of the futurist scenario failing over and over again. But, in the meantime, I began to study other possibilities. Of course, to this day, the book of Revelation remains the undisputed most controversial book in the Bible for interpreting—and the most enigmatic.

The Importance of Revelation

I actually got to the point where I stopped reading Revelation because so many Christians disagreed on the details. If I couldn't be sure who was right, why waste my short life speculating about uncertainties when the rest of the New Testament was so clear about our primary purpose on earth: preach the gospel to the lost and pursue the kingdom of God. Endless speculation about the future seemed to be a sidetrack to what was most important. No matter what happened in the near future regarding the Antichrist, everyone still needed to get right with the true Christ before the final judgment. Redemption was so much more about living our spiritual life here and now, rather than focusing on a sensational theory that has yet to happen.

I now believe that such avoidance of a book of Scripture is detrimental to spiritual growth. Not only does the book itself promise a blessing on those who read it and keep what is written in it (Rev 1:3), but ignoring one part of God's Word because it's difficult or ambiguous is to restrict yourself from the fullness of what God considers important enough to have included in the sacred canon. "All Scripture is breathed out by God and profitable for teaching, for reproof, for correction, and for training in righteousness, that the man of God may be complete, equipped for every good work" (2 Tim 3:16–17). Not only that, but the book of Revelation is so important to God that he curses anyone who changes the words in it (Rev 22:18).

The depths of God in Scripture are not encountered without diligent study and hard work. It's the same for any form of maturity or growth.

Children don't want to work for maturity. They want it handed to them like candy. Adults know that you cannot grow or understand the deeper things of life without struggling with them and enduring.

But at the time I did consider there to be other, more clear passages in the New Testament that spoke of this end of days timeline. So I focused on those in my attempt to clarify the issues. And one of the most powerful and obvious passages of prophecy was Jesus' Olivet Discourse recorded in Matthew 24, Mark 13, and Luke 21. I mean, if Jesus Christ himself told us clearly what was going to happen at the end of the age, we certainly have a convincing argument directly from the Master's mouth. In it Jesus covered just about everything I referred to in my end times Bible chart: the rapture (Matt 24:40-41), the great tribulation (v. 21), the Antichrist (v. 15), cosmic catastrophes (v. 29), and the second coming (v. 30). It read like a virtual summary of the book of Revelation!

Believe it or not, the Olivet Discourse was actually the doorway for me to change my views of the end times from that popular, futurist interpretation to a preterist one. Futurism teaches that the last days prophecies are all in our current future; whereas, preterism teaches that most of those prophecies were actually fulfilled in the past. The word *preterism* is Latin in origin and it means "past."

What? These prophesies already fulfilled in the past? Heresy! I told you before, that's exactly how I reacted. But if you have an open mind and are willing to put in some real consideration of ancient scriptures (as opposed to modern newspapers), you may find yourself with the same stone in your shoe that I received: a nagging respect that soon grew into a full-fledged embrace of a beautiful truth about the new covenant that I was missing out on.

Because this was the passage that changed my mind, this will be the passage I want to walk you through in explaining what I believe the last days is really all about. I will only touch on some things from the book of Revelation, but will not have the time or space to address it in detail here. Check out the bibliography at the back of this book for recommendations of scholarly works on the book of Revelation. They will blow your mind and open up the Word of God in amazing and fresh ways.

Chapter 7
O Jerusalem, Jerusalem!

Matthew 24 is commonly known as the Olivet Discourse. It was a sermon that Jesus gave to his disciples on the Mount of Olives outside Jerusalem just two days before he was betrayed and delivered up to be crucified (Matt 26:1). It is a key chapter in understanding end times Bible prophecy because it comes from the lips of Jesus himself. But rather than start with verse 1, it is more important to start with chapter 23, which sets the stage and the context for everything Jesus said in chapter 24.

Matthew 23 places Jesus in the temple, proclaiming seven woes upon the scribes and Pharisees, the religious leaders of Israel. These are the kind of things that have now become cliché to us in connection with the term *Pharisaism*: hypocrisy, religious fraud, legalism, the blind leading the blind. But it is important to remember that in that day Pharisees were not a condemned class as they are now. Back then they were considered genuine and respectable because they enforced rigid dedication to the law of God. And they were leaders who represented the people before God.

Judaism was a representative theocracy; that is to say, God ruled through the leaders. Much like a representative republic, those in authority represented the people at large. If the authorities were righteous—be they prophet, priest, or king—God would bless them along with the people. If the authorities were corrupt, God would punish them along with his people. This is the principle behind the federal headship or federal representation of Adam and Christ in Romans 5:2-21. Unbelievers are "in Adam," or represented by his rebellion and curse. But when they place their faith in Jesus, they become "in Christ," or represented by him and therefore receivers of the benefits of his righteousness.

This notion of Jewish federal representation is important because the condemnation of the Jewish leaders by Jesus was not exclusively aimed at them. We will see in the text that the people followed them in that condemnation. The final woe from Jesus is the worst judgment of all. The Jewish leaders, and by extension the Jewish people, became guilty of the worst crime in all history: the rejection of God's representatives, the prophets, and ultimately the rejection of their own Messiah. Here is what Jesus actually said of them.

> Matthew 23:29–39
> Woe to you, scribes and Pharisees, hypocrites! For you build the tombs of the prophets and decorate the monuments of the righteous, [30] saying, "If we had lived in the days of our fathers, we would not have taken part with them in shedding the blood of the prophets." [31] Thus you witness against yourselves that you are sons of those who murdered the prophets. [32] Fill up, then, the measure of your fathers. [33] You serpents, you brood of vipers, how are you to escape being sentenced to hell? [34] Therefore I send you prophets and wise men and scribes, some of whom you will kill and crucify, and some you will flog in your synagogues and persecute from town to town, [35] so that on you may come all the righteous blood shed on earth, from the blood of righteous Abel to the blood of Zechariah the son of Barachiah, whom you murdered between the sanctuary and the altar. [36] Truly, I say to you, all these things will come upon this generation. [37] O Jerusalem, Jerusalem, the city that kills the prophets and stones those who are sent to it! How often would I have gathered your children together as a hen gathers her brood under her wings, and you were not willing! [38] See, your house is left to you desolate. [39] For I tell you, you will not see me again, until you say, "Blessed is he who comes in the name of the Lord." 24[1] Jesus left the temple and was going away, when his disciples came to point out to him the buildings of the temple. [2] But he answered them, "You see all these, do you not? Truly, I say to you, there will not be left here one stone upon another that will not be thrown down."

Notice the two sentences I underlined, verses 35 and 36. In this fiery damnation, Jesus said that his own generation of Jews and their leaders would be judicially guilty before God of all the murders of the righteous men and prophets in their history. You read that right—guilty of all the righteous blood shed on earth. That's pretty much the highest guilt and condemnation that anyone can have. Isn't that rather extreme of God to blame that single, first century generation for everybody else's crimes?

Remember, this is a spiritual reality of representation. In other passages Jesus explained this principle. His generation received all the blame of God's condemnation because they rejected the highest of all prophets and righteous men, the one that is God himself—the Messiah. And because of this highest of high-handed crimes, they would receive the highest punishment, the absolute destruction of their holy temple ("your house") that represented their covenant relationship with God.

Think about that for a moment. The holy temple was the heart and soul of Israel. It was the house of God where the priests atoned for sin and brought the people back into right relationship with God. The inner temple contained the Holy of Holies where God's throne and ark of the covenant resided. The ark was the footstool of his throne on earth. This was the earthly dwelling of God among his people. The temple and its sacrificial system was the incarnation of their covenant with God, and Jesus was prophesying that God was going to obliterate that symbol and, along with it, the covenant.

But how could that be? I thought the Jews were God's chosen people forever. I thought their calling was irrevocable and unconditional. I thought God always forgives.

Well, I thought wrong.

The Parable of the Tenants

In Matthew 21, Jesus told the parable of the tenants, a reiteration and extension of Isaiah's parable of the vineyard (Isa 5). God is likened to a master who plants a vineyard, a metaphor for the kingdom of God (as are all his parables). The Jews are likened to tenants that the master leases the vineyard to. But when the master/God sends his servants/the prophets to get the fruit, the tenants/the Jews kill them all. Finally, when the master sends his son/Jesus, the tenants/the Jews kill him as well, desiring to take his inheritance. Jesus then asked his audience the question, "When therefore the owner of the vineyard comes, what will he do to those tenants?" The audience responded, "He will put those wretches to a miserable death and let out the vineyard to other tenants who will give him the fruits in their seasons" (v. 41). Did you read that? He kills them and leases the vineyard to *other tenants*. Jesus then quoted a messianic Psalm.

> Matthew 21:42–44
> Have you never read in the Scriptures: "The stone that the builders rejected has become the cornerstone; this was the Lord's doing, and it is marvelous in our eyes"? [43] Therefore I tell you, the kingdom of God will be taken away from you and given to a people producing its fruits. [44] And the one who falls on this stone will be broken to pieces; and when it falls on anyone, it will crush him.

I had previously thought that this parable was about the second coming of Christ. You know, all that talk about when the owner of the vineyard returns sounds similar to the return of Christ. But this was my modern bias blinding me to the ancient context, because the context is actually about the *first* coming of Christ, not the second.

N.T. Wright has written extensively about how the Jews had expected God to return to Zion and rescue them. And that return was the arrival of the promised Messiah![1] But Jesus was saying that God was returning all right, in the form of Messiah, but he was not going to rescue, but rather to judge! Why? Because when that generation of Jews rejected their Messiah, they rejected God himself. Wright quoted R.B. Caird in saying,

> Jesus believed that Israel was called by God to be the agent of his purpose, and that he himself had been sent to bring about that reformation without which Israel could not fulfill her national destiny. If the nation, so far from accepting that calling, rejected God's messenger and persecuted those who responded to his preaching, how could the assertion of

[1] N. T. Wright, *The New Testament and the People of God*, Christian Origins and the Question of God. (London: Society for Promoting Christian Knowledge, 1992).

> God's sovereignty fail to include an open demonstration that Jesus was right and the nation was wrong? How could it fail to include the vindication of the persecuted and the cause they lived and died for?[2]

In the parable of the tenants, Jesus made a messianic temple reference to himself as the rejected cornerstone of the holy temple of God, a quotation from Psalm 118. In Ephesians 2, we read that Jesus is the cornerstone of the new temple of God, a spiritual temple of the new covenant.

> Ephesians 2:19–22
> You are fellow citizens with the saints and members of the household of God, [20] built on the foundation of the apostles and prophets, Christ Jesus himself being the cornerstone, [21] in whom the whole structure, being joined together, grows into a holy temple in the Lord. [22] In him you also are being built together into a dwelling place for God by the Spirit.

Paul reiterated this new covenant spiritual temple of the body of Christ in 1 Corinthians 6:16 where he wrote, "We are the temple of the living God; as God said, 'I will make my dwelling among them and walk with them, and I will be their God, and they shall be my people.'" Peter affirmed the picture of the church as the new spiritual temple with Christ as its cornerstone and Christians as the spiritual stones of that temple.

> 1 Peter 2:4–6
> As you come to him, a living stone rejected by men but in the sight of God chosen and precious, [5] you yourselves like living stones are being built up as a spiritual house, to be a holy priesthood, to offer spiritual sacrifices acceptable to God through Jesus Christ. [6] For it stands in Scripture: "Behold, I am laying in Zion a stone, a cornerstone chosen and precious, and whoever believes in him will not be put to shame."

---

[2] N. T. Wright, *Jesus and the Victory of God*, Christian Origins and the Question of God (London: Society for Promoting Christian Knowledge, 1996), 320.

So going back to the parable of the tenants, Jesus concluded that those who reject him, the cornerstone of the new temple, will be "crushed" by his judgment (21:44). This was not the final judgment at the end of history; this prophecy of the destruction of the temple and Jerusalem was fulfilled in A.D. 70 by the Roman forces of Titus. When I learned this amazing historical fulfillment, I was bothered by the fact that none of the Bible prophecy teachers taught about this most important prophetic fulfillment. Or, at best, they mentioned it briefly and moved on to what they thought was the really important prophecies of the end times. As it turns out, there is an account of this Roman siege of Jerusalem that ended in its destruction. It is called *The Wars of the Jews*, written by Jewish historian Flavius Josephus, who actually participated in the historic events. Learning about that event opened my eyes even more. The destruction of Jerusalem and the temple is the very beginning of Jesus' Olivet Discourse and is the very heart and soul of the entire discourse from Matthew chapters 23 and 24. And in the parable of the tenants, we see that same motif of judgment and temple destruction.

But that is not all. When Jesus said that God would judge the original tenants and then "let out the vineyard to other tenants who will give him the fruits in their seasons," just who exactly was he talking about? Since the vineyard is a metaphor for the kingdom of God, Jesus was saying that he was going to give that kingdom to another people. The original tenants were only tenants after all, not owners.

Just who are these people who were not God's original people but are given the responsibility of his kingdom in the new covenant? Romans chapter 9 fills out the explanation in its inclusion of the Gentiles and the exclusion of unbelieving Israel. In that chapter Paul explained the nature of election and how God chooses whomever he wants to be his chosen people. He answered an objection that this seems unfair by explaining that God owes nothing to a wicked world of sinners. God can choose some for his blessing and others for wrath and destruction, since we all deserve destruction anyway.

Then comes his climactic point. He quotes the Old Testament prophet Hosea, who spoke for God, saying, "Those who were not my people I will call 'my people,' and her who was not beloved I will call 'beloved.'" "And in the very place where it was said to them, 'You are not my people,' there they will be called 'sons of the living God'" (9:25-26).

Paul was talking about the Gentiles becoming God's people through faith, those new people that Jesus said in the parable of the tenants would produce the fruit of the vineyard. Why? Because the new covenant clarifies that righteousness is not based on physical genetics or geopolitical land; it is based on faith.

> Romans 9:30–33
> What shall we say, then? That Gentiles who did not pursue righteousness have attained it, that is, a righteousness that is by faith; [31] but that Israel who pursued a law that would lead to righteousness did not succeed in reaching that law. [32] Why? Because they did not pursue it by faith, but as if it were based on works. They have stumbled over the stumbling stone, [33] as it is written, "Behold, I am laying in Zion a stone of stumbling, and a rock of offense; and whoever believes in him will not be put to shame."

There it is again—that reference to Jesus as the cornerstone of a new temple and God's rejection and judgment of unbelieving Jews replaced by a new people. The stone would crush whomever was not broken upon it (Matt 21:44).

Does this mean that God has replaced all Jews with Gentiles, or Israel with the church? By no means. Paul was making a theological comparison to stress God's rejection of unbelieving Israel, as represented by her unbelieving leaders (federal representation). The problem is that sometimes the term *Israel* is used in the specific sense of the political nation state, and other times it is used in its more generic sense, meaning the people of God as opposed to that nation state (Rom 9:6). Still other times, *Israel* is used to mean exclusively unbelieving Jews in contrast with all believers (Gal 6:16). As I have already established in this book, context always determines meaning and that meaning is not always obvious. So in this Romans 9 passage, Paul used *Israel* in its specific reference to unbelieving Jews. Elsewhere Paul wrote that true Israel consists of believing Jews and Gentiles alike, while excluding unbelieving Jews (Rom 2:28-29; 11:11-24; Eph 3:6).

In that sense, the new people Jesus was giving his kingdom to (Matt 21:43) would be a people not rooted in a specific land like geopolitical Israel, but from all over the earth, a strange new people that included Gentiles along with believing Jews.

This raises all kinds of questions about the meaning of *Israel* and the eternal promise to Abraham and Abraham's children, as well as accusations of so-called replacement theology. I have addressed all of these issues in my free booklet entitled "Israel in Bible Prophecy: The New Testament Fulfillment of the Promise to Abraham," available for purchase at online bookstores or for free when you sign up for the free booklet at the beginning of this book (Matthew 24 Fulfilled).

The main point here is that both Jesus and Paul did refer to the geopolitical nation state of Israel with its temple as the center of God's will, *but for judgment, not redemption.* Jesus was not going to save geopolitical Israel; he was going to judge her, divorce her in God's spiritual court of law.[3] Going back now to Matthew 23 and 24, Jesus prophesied that his generation would reject him as Messiah, so they would be rejected by God. God would destroy the temple, the symbol of the old covenant and create a new spiritual temple with Jesus as the messianic cornerstone of that new covenant.

Whispers of Anti-Semitism

When I was first faced with this reality of God's utter rejection and judgment of the Jews, I was deeply disturbed. I mean it was virtually an inversion of everything I had been told about end times prophecy and the importance of Israel as the darling of that big, detailed Bible chart of the last days. My dispensational instinct kicked in, along with the accusations I was conditioned to assume. Wasn't blaming Jews for the crucifixion of Jesus the root of anti-Semitism? Didn't the Crusades and other anti-Semitic atrocities of history use that very accusation of Jews as Christ killers to justify genocide and holocaust? In fact, Hal Lindsey, that first and foremost influence on me, actually wrote a book about it called *The Road to*

---

[3] For the full theological treatment of God's divorce of Israel see, Kenneth L. Gentry, Jr., *The Divorce of Israel: A Redemptive-Historical Interpretation of Revelation*, (Dallas, GA: Tolle Lege Press, 2016).

Holocaust. Sadly, Lindsey and his more recent successors continue to make these claims today.

These were serious ramifications. I don't even want a hint of connection to any racist hatred. And I would never in a million years want to find myself cursing what God has blessed. But neither would I want to find myself blessing what God has cursed. So I looked deeper. And sadly, it didn't take much biblical depth at all to dispel the accusation of anti-Semitism as slanderous.

It Just Doesn't Follow

The first error of this slander of anti-Semitism is that it is a *non sequitur*, the conclusion doesn't logically follow from the premise. If the Jews as a group are guilty of a crime before God, that does not mean that other sinful humans are allowed to kill them. Criminals are the biggest blame shifters of humanity. They always make up reasons to rationalize their evil behavior. Even if the Jews of that generation were guilty for crucifying Christ, it wouldn't follow that therefore anyone can go and kill Jews. That would be a *non sequitur* and the Bible says no such thing.

Those who conclude that Jews are more evil than other sinners before God, or that they deserve to be persecuted or harmed because they killed the Christ, are not only illogical and unscriptural but also evil rebels against God and persecutors who deserve to be judged by God.

Who Killed Christ?

The second fallacy of the anti-Semitic accusation against preterism is the false generalization that if you indict some of a people group, you are therefore indicting all of that people group. The view I am arguing for does not claim that all Jews through all history are Christ killers. It does not say that all the blood of all the righteous shed on the earth is on the heads of all Jews through all history. The view was explicitly stated by Jesus that *his generation* that rejected the arrival of Messiah was the one guilty of all the bloodshed (and of being the climactic offspring of a history of rejecting God). *That* generation of the first century would experience the destruction of Jerusalem and the temple, not future generations. Of course, it is theologically true that all unbelievers, Jew and Gentile alike, are guilty and deserving of God's judgment if they reject Jesus as Messiah. But that is a different issue than the prophecy of Matthew 23-24 of the historical judgment on the temple.

A third fallacy against preterism lies in the objection that the Jews didn't kill Christ; the Romans did. Oh, really? So accessories to murder are not guilty of murder? In a just legal system like God's law, they sure are. Listen to what Peter, a Jew with apostolic authority, said about who was guilty of killing Jesus.

> Acts 2:22–23
> Men of Israel, hear these words: …this Jesus, delivered up according to the definite plan and foreknowledge of God, you crucified and killed by the hands of lawless men.

Yes, the Romans, those "lawless men," were the hands that killed Christ. But the Jews who delivered him over to the Romans were considered equally guilty of that crime, even so far as saying that they killed Christ "by the hands" of others.

In two other proclamations in Acts, Peter reiterated this theme of bloodguilt on his first century countrymen.

> Acts 3:13–15
> The God of Abraham, the God of Isaac, and the God of Jacob, the God of our fathers, glorified his servant Jesus, whom you delivered over and denied in the presence of Pilate, when he had decided to release him. [14] But you denied the Holy and Righteous One, and asked for a murderer to be granted to you, [15] and you killed the Author of life, whom God raised from the dead. To this we are witnesses.

> Acts 5:30–31
> The God of our fathers raised Jesus, whom you killed by hanging him on a tree. [31] God exalted him at his right hand as Leader and Savior, to give repentance to Israel and forgiveness of sins.

Peter clearly placed the guilt of killing Messiah on the same people that Jesus did, those first century Jews who killed Messiah. Even though the Romans technically carried out the deed, God said that the apostle's own Jewish people also denied God's Holy and Righteous One, also killed the Author of Life, and also hung him on a tree.

The apostle Paul agreed with Peter when he wrote about the Jews persecuting Christians in his day.

> 1 Thessalonians 2:14–16
> For you, brothers… suffered the same things from your own countrymen as they did from the Jews, [15] who killed both the Lord Jesus and the prophets, and drove us out, and displease God and oppose all mankind [16] by hindering us from speaking to the Gentiles that they might be saved—so as always to fill up the measure of their sins. But wrath has come upon them at last!

Here, Paul, who wrote most of the New Testament, accused the Jews of killing both Jesus and the prophets—just like Jesus said in Matthew 23! Paul even concurred with Jesus that wrath was about to come upon the Jews: the destruction of the temple and their dispersion into all the nations.

So the apostles, who are the foundation of our faith (Eph 2:20), with the authority of God himself, accused their own brethren, the Jews of their generation, of killing Christ. Which brings me to the final point.

Will the Real Anti-Semite Please Stand Up?

The most egregious error of dispensational accusers of preterism as being anti-Semitic is that those same futurists are in the unenviable position of accusing God and his prophets of being anti-Semitic. I've already shown that the two key apostles, Peter and Paul, were themselves Jews and yet they condemned the Jews for rejecting Messiah. But you need go no further than pointing out that it was Jesus, the *Jewish* Messiah, God in the flesh, who condemned that generation of Jews for their ultimate act of killing him. Those of us who seek to be faithful to the text are merely repeating what Jesus the Christ said of his murderers. God condemned that generation, not us. So, please, don't martyr the messenger.

And those *Jewish* apostles and their *Jewish* Messiah were simply reiterating a long history of condemnation of the Jewish people for apostasy from God—*by the Jewish prophets of Israel*—who were themselves echoing God's own sentiments!

Ezekiel, speaking for God, likened Israel to the offspring of godless pagans. He called Israel an adulterous whore who had abominable sex with other gods and their followers (Ezek 16). Similar to Jesus' prophecy of temple desolation, Ezekiel pronounced God's message of the first desolation of the temple by the Babylonians.

> Ezekiel 23:28–35
> For thus says the Lord GOD: ...your [Israel's] lewdness and your whoring [30] have brought this upon you, because you played the whore with the nations and defiled yourself with their idols...[35] Therefore thus says the Lord GOD: Because you have forgotten me and cast me behind your back, you yourself must bear the consequences of your lewdness and whoring.

Bible scholar Kenneth L. Gentry in a commentary on Revelation gave a few more examples of the condemnation of Israel by Old Testament prophets.

> Isaiah castigates Israel: "Alas, sinful nation, / People weighed down with iniquity, / Offspring of evildoers, / Sons who act corruptly! / They have abandoned the Lord, / They have despised the Holy One of Israel, / They have turned away from Him" (Isa 1:4). He calls her leaders "rulers of Sodom" and her people "people of Gomorrah" (Isa 1:10), much like John does in Rev 11:8. In Isa 10:5–6 God sends Assyria against Israel because she is a "godless nation." In fact, he scathingly derides the temple in his day: "he who kills an ox is like one who slays a man; / He who sacrifices a lamb is like the one who breaks a dog's neck; / He who offers a grain offering is like one who offers swine's blood; / He who burns incense is like the one who blesses an idol. / As they have chosen their own ways, / And their soul

> delights in their abominations." (Isaiah 66:3) And Amos 9:7 deems "the sons of Israel" as "the sons of Ethiopia." Were not Isaiah and Amos Jews, writing in Israel's Bible? Were they anti-Semitic? Must we remove Isaiah and Amos from Scripture so that true anti-Semites will not use it?
>
> Jeremiah calls Jerusalem a harlot (as does John in Rev!): "You are a harlot with many lovers... You have a polluted land" (Jer 3:1, 2). "I saw that for all the adulteries of faithless Israel, I had sent her away and given her a writ of divorce, yet her treacherous sister Judah did not fear; but she went and was a harlot also" (Jer 3:8). Was Jeremiah the Jew, a contributor to Jewish Scripture, and a beloved prophet of Israel, speaking in a way that we may condemn as anti-Semitic?[4]

I could go on and on with a litany of these examples from every single Old Testament prophet condemning Israel for faithless rejection of God. These prophetic judgments came directly from God and included a call to repentance and renewed faith. But Israel as a nation was guilty before God. To call such proclamations anti-Semitic would be to call God himself anti-Semitic. Would anyone really want to place themselves in such a foolish and dangerous position?

The Parables of Jesus

This context of condemnation for the first century Jews brings new light on the darkened understanding of Jesus' other parables of the kingdom.

Most Christians misread Jesus' parables as generic references to judgment or specific parables about his second coming. But they are not. They are parables about the *first* coming of Messiah. They are not about the final judgment at the end of time, but about the localized judgment in the first century. They reinforce the covenant lawsuit theme that God would judge the people who would reject Messiah. It marks the coming end of the

---

[4] Kenneth L. Gentry, Jr., "XXII. Anti-Semitism Charges," *The Divorce of Israel: A Redemptive-Historical Interpretation of Revelation,* (Dallas, GA: Tolle Lege Press, 2016), unpublished manuscript.

old covenant and the replacement of it with a new covenant and new covenant people.

Try rereading those parables with that new, first century context and you may see the power of the ancient paradigm open your eyes. A recommended resource that helps explain this is Joel McDurmon's *Jesus v. Jerusalem: A Commentary on Luke 9:51–20:26, Jesus' Lawsuit Against Israel.*[5]

One Last Little "Big" Thing

Many dispensationalists and other futurists believe that, according to Zechariah 13:8, under the future rule of the Antichrist, two-thirds of the Jews in the land of Israel will perish. These same dispensationalists also support modern Jews returning to Israel to claim that territory, using God's authority over the land. So in other words, they are encouraging Jews to return to the land that they believe will result in two-thirds of those Jews being slaughtered by the Antichrist.

Just who is the real anti-Semite here?

---

[5] Joel McDurmon, *Jesus v. Jerusalem: A Commentary on Luke 9:51–20:26, Jesus' Lawsuit Against Israel* (Georgia, American Vision, 2011).

Chapter 8
This Generation

In the previous chapter, we saw how Jesus condemned the generation of his hearers in Matthew 23:36 for their rejection of God. But there is another aspect of that phrase he used, "this generation," that would become the biggest stone in my shoe, eventually leading me to change my entire view of the last days. There was something about that phrase—"Truly, I say to you, all these things will come upon this generation"—that would haunt my eschatology to such a degree that it would lead me to completely reverse everything I had previously believed about this prophetic discourse on the Mount of Olives. This single time reference, all by itself, began to unravel the futurist end times view that had held me for so long. It was the stone in my shoe that became the cornerstone of my new temple view.

Look closer at that verse: Jesus said, "Truly, I say to you, all these things will come upon this generation." What things? Jesus had just condemned them in chapter 23 with the bloodguilt of killing the prophets and, ultimately, the Christ. He said that the guilt would be upon them. That bloodguilt would lead to the things Jesus was describing. So, what things was he describing? Right after this prediction, he said the temple would be desolated (23:38). But that is only one thing; that is not "things," plural. Now, it could be another way of saying that the killing of the prophets would be upon this generation as bloodguilt. But then what is the point of guilt without punishment? The guilt leads to the punishment of temple and city destruction. Right after this, Jesus left the temple and reiterated that the temple would be completely destroyed, down to the last stone. He went up to the Mount of Olives where his disciples asked in response to this predicted judgment, "Tell us, when will these things be, and what will be the sign of your coming and of the end of the age?"

Jesus then proceeded to predict many things that would lead to the destruction of the city and temple that they were asking about. Wars, tribulation, persecution, the abomination of desolation, and other things, all the way up to and including his "coming on the clouds of heaven." Then at the end of that discourse of judgments, he said something that is the lynchpin of interpretation of "these things": he repeated the phrase, "Truly, I say to you, this generation will not pass away until all these things take place."

It is like a pair of bookends or parentheses that includes everything between them as the answer to the question. By repeating that key phrase about *his generation*, Jesus was affirming that everything *after* the first mention and *before* the second mention would take place on "this generation." "All these things." Not some of them, all of them. That means even the coming of the Son of Man, because the coming of the Son of Man is within those bookends or parentheses!

When I first understood this implication, I balked. Why that couldn't possibly be true, because the Son of Man hasn't come yet. Neither has the abomination of desolation. The stars haven't fallen from heaven, nor the powers of the heavens shaken.

Or have they? Was I imposing my own interpretation upon the text rather than letting the text guide my interpretation of the details?

Now, as we found out earlier, it is possible that "all" does not mean all, if the context indicates hyperbole. But in this case, there is no poetic equivalent of "all these things" to "all the nations." The context supports the simple, straightforward time reference, just as the time texts of the day of the Lord being "near" were straightforward in the past.

This raises the issue of an important rule of biblical hermeneutics or proper interpretation of Scriptures. *Sola scriptura* is the principle that the scriptures are the final authority of the truth. We are to let Scripture interpret Scripture. So whenever Scripture contradicts what we think is true, our interpretation must be adjusted to accord with what the Bible says. It would not be appropriate to adjust what the Bible says to fit our understanding. As I already showed in the first section of this book, we modern readers often assume that the cosmic catastrophes of the sun, moon, and stars going dark means literal astronomical fallout. It seems self-evident until we find out that cosmic catastrophes were a well-known poetic way of saying the fall of ruling earthly and heavenly authorities. Their lights would go out because they would lose their power. It seems evident to us that the day of the Lord means the single, universal final judgment at the end of history until we find out that "day of the Lord" was a poetic way that ancient Hebrews described God judging many different local cities, peoples, and nations at different times.

If this interpretive principle of prioritizing the ancient mindset and poetic language of the Jews is true, then the reader can easily see the folly of saying, "All these things could not have taken place, because the abomination of desolation hasn't happened, or the great tribulation hasn't happened." That would be begging the question. The question is exactly what are the abomination of desolation and the great tribulation? Are they what we think they should be in our Western mindset and thought forms, or are they what the ancient text, *in context,* says they mean *within their mindset, using their thought forms*? If Jesus himself said that *all these things* would take place before his generation would pass away and that all these things would come upon his generation, then we must interpret everything within those brackets as having taken place upon *them* before *his* generation passed away. Otherwise, we are changing Jesus's words to fit our preconceived notions. We are imposing our predetermined theological bias upon the text. We must adjust our *interpretation* of what the abomination of desolation is and what the great tribulation is—and yes, even what the coming of the Son of Man is—to fit Jesus' ancient meaning, not the other way around.

Who Is This Generation?

Many futurists see this dilemma and seek to reinterpret the meaning of "this generation," so that everything will fit their eschatological paradigm. They will abandon their literalism for figurative language here (once again, proving that nobody interprets all Bible prophecy literally. Nobody). They will say, *generation* means "race of the Jews." The Jewish race would not pass away until all these things take place. Since the Jewish race has not passed away and it is now the 21st century, then all these things are yet to happen in our future. Others will say that Jesus was not really talking to his contemporaries, but rather he was speaking to a future generation. He was saying that a future generation *that would see these signs* would not pass away. That future generation could be ours or a generation future to ours.

There are several problems with these futurist interpretations of "this generation" that invalidate them on biblical grounds. First, the Greek word for "generation" that Jesus used is *genea.* The Louw-Nida Greek-English Lexicon explains, "The expression 'the people of this generation' may also be expressed as 'the people living now' or 'the people of this time.'"[1] It simply doesn't mean "the Jewish race" anywhere in the New Testament. In fact, I looked up all the places where that phrase "this generation" is used by Jesus in the Gospels, and, lo and behold, he always used it to clearly refer to the generation of people he was speaking to.

But that's not all. He also used that reference to "generation" in the same way he was using it in Matthew 23 and 24; he was calling judgment down upon his current generation what would reject him as Messiah!

Here is a listing of all the places Jesus used that concept *this generation.* Notice the context of judgment that matches Matthew 23 and 24. Resist the temptation to glide over these verses. Read each of them to let the impact of this powerful truth sink in, as it did for me.

> Matthew 11:16 (Luke 7:31)
> But to what shall I compare this generation? It is like children sitting in the marketplaces and calling to their playmates.
>
> Matthew 12:39 (Mark 8:12; Luke 11:29)
> An evil and adulterous generation seeks for a sign, but no sign will be given to it except the sign of the prophet Jonah.
>
> Matthew 12:41 (Luke 11:32)
> The men of Nineveh will rise up at the judgment with this generation and condemn it, for they repented at the preaching of Jonah, and behold, something greater than Jonah is here.
>
> Matthew 12:42 (Luke 11:31)
> The queen of the South will rise up at the judgment with this generation and condemn it, for she came from the ends of

[1] Johannes P. Louw and Eugene Albert Nida, *Greek-English Lexicon of the New Testament: Based on Semantic Domains* (New York: United Bible Societies, 1996), 119.

the earth to hear the wisdom of Solomon, and behold, something greater than Solomon is here.

Matthew 12:45
Then it goes and brings with it seven other spirits more evil than itself, and they enter and dwell there, and the last state of that person is worse than the first. So also will it be with this evil generation.

Matthew 16:4
An evil and adulterous generation seeks for a sign, but no sign will be given to it except the sign of Jonah. So he left them and departed.

Matthew 17:17 (Mark 9:19; Luke 9:41)
O faithless and twisted generation, how long am I to be with you? How long am I to bear with you?

Matthew 23:36
Truly, I say to you, all these things will come upon this generation.

Luke 11:50-52
so that the blood of all the prophets, shed from the foundation of the world, may be charged against this generation, from the blood of Abel to the blood of Zechariah, who perished between the altar and the sanctuary. Yes, I tell you, it will be required of this generation.

Matthew 24:34 (Mark 13:30; Luke 21:32)
Truly, I say to you, this generation will not pass away until all these things take place.

Mark 8:38
For whoever is ashamed of me and of my words in this adulterous and sinful generation, of him will the Son of Man also be ashamed when he comes in the glory of his Father with the holy angels.

> Luke 11:30
> For as Jonah became a sign to the people of Nineveh, so will the Son of Man be to this generation.

> Luke 16:8
> The master commended the dishonest manager for his shrewdness. For the sons of this world are more shrewd in dealing with their own generation than the sons of light.

> Luke 17:25
> But first he must suffer many things and be rejected by this generation.

A Generation of Guilt

Do you see the clear pattern in Jesus' preaching? Not only did he always mean the generation he was speaking to when he said "this generation," but in every instance he used it in reference to the judgment that would come upon them for rejecting the promised Messiah! He repeated it over and over so many times that it was clearly a most significant part of his ministry to condemn those of his generation.

And the apostles preached the same judgment upon that generation that Jesus did.

> Acts 2:40
> [Peter] bore witness and continued to exhort them, saying, "Save yourselves from this crooked generation."

> Acts 8:33
> [Philip:] In [Jesus'] humiliation justice was denied him. Who can describe his generation? For his life is taken away from the earth.

There is no future generation that would see these signs. The generation that saw the signs was the same generation that was being judged for rejecting Messiah, and that generation was the generation Jesus was speaking to.

Chapter 9
End of the Age / Last Days

So, I've established the fact that the entire purpose of Matthew 23 is to set up the guilt of the first century generation of the Jews for rejecting and killing their own Messiah. God then said he would destroy "their house," the temple, which he no longer considered his house.

At this point in studying the text, I learned another blindness of my modern bias in Bible reading. The chapter headings are not in the original text of the Bible. Well-meaning medieval monks put them there for easy referencing. Fair enough. But the problem is that this breaking up of the text creates the false picture of completed units of thought. It is as if chapter 23 ends and now the writer is going to talk about a new subject in chapter 24. Not so. Matthew's Gospel is one flowing storyline with units larger than chapters. Chapter 23 flows out of a series of prior paragraphs that pit the scribes and Pharisees against Jesus. When Jesus condemned the Jewish leaders in 23, it was in response to all the chapters of confrontations that precede it. And chapter 24 is a continuation of the chapter 23 condemnation. The context of chapter 24 is the judgment upon those Jews who would reject Jesus as Messiah. So chapter 24 is nothing less than the description of what that judgment upon Israel would look like. Matthew 23: God is going to destroy your house (the temple); Matthew 24: this is how it will happen.

But this was where I got flummoxed. Don't the very first verses of chapter 24 place Jesus and the disciples on the Mount of Olives, a different location than the temple where he declared the judgment? Yes, but in storytelling, just as in movies, scenes or locations can change without changing the context or the discussion. Look at what they asked him: "Tell us, when will these things be, and what will be the sign of your coming and of the end of the age?" (Matt 24:3).

What are "these things" other than the very things Jesus was telling them in the previous verses of chapter 23? (Remember, it's technically not a chapter but a continuing story.)

It was at this point that some Bible teachers taught me that the disciples' question involved three different things: (1) the things of judgment in chapter 23 and 24, (2) Christ's coming, and (3) the end of the age. I was taught that they are all different, unconnected events. The problem is that the context of the discourse does not support this theory. It is a very common poetic device for Scripture to speak of the same event or the same thing with multiple phrases or parallels.

For instance, when Simeon prophesied over young Jesus in the temple, he said, "Behold, this child is appointed for the fall and rising of many in Israel, and for a sign that is opposed (and a sword will pierce through your own soul also), so that thoughts from many hearts may be revealed" (Luke 2:34–35). These three things— (1) the fall and rise of many in Israel, (2) a sign that is opposed, and (3) a sword will pierce your own heart—are all separate things; but they are all different elements of the one event of Jesus Christ appointed as Messiah.

In the same way, when the disciples asked Jesus in Matthew 24:3 about these things—his coming and the end of the age—they saw them all as one packaged event with several aspects to it. I will be arguing next that the context of the discourse is the destruction of the temple ("these things"), which was rooted in the end of the old covenant ("age") and embodied in Christ spiritually coming in judgment upon Israel in the first century in the form of temple destruction.

Shocking, yes, I know. It shocked me at first too. But follow me on this. I had always assumed that when Jesus referred to his "coming," it was his second coming at the end of history. I was amazed to discover that this was not necessarily the case. But that revelation will be examined in the next chapter of this book. First, let me show you how I learned what the end of the age or the last days really means.

End of the Age

I had always been taught that the end of the age was the end of history, the end of the world, and the final judgment of mankind. Surely such language was obvious in its huge scope. But remember what we have learned about the Old Testament imagery of worldwide and cosmic language used of covenants? Well, consider this: Jesus and the writers of the New Testament were ancient Jews steeped in the Old Testament, its imagery, language, and poetry. They were not modern, scientific Westerners like you and I. As I looked into the concept of the end of the age and the last days, I discovered a covenantal meaning that blew my mind.

My first hint was that the Greek word for "age" that Jesus used was *aion*, which Louw-Nida defines as "a unit of time as a particular stage or period of history—age, era."[1]

This notion of the end of the age shows up in other teachings from Jesus. At the end of Matthew, Jesus said to his disciples, "Behold, I am with you always, to the end of the age" (28:20). In another place he said that those who followed him would receive both persecutions and spiritual family in this age, "and in the age to come eternal life" (Mark 10:30).

The notion of the present age and the messianic age to come was prevalent in Jewish understanding and in the New Testament as well. Paul wrote of the Christians living in "this age" (1 Cor 3:18), "this present evil age" (Gal 1:4) that had evil spiritual rulers of this age (1 Cor 2:8; 2 Cor 4:4); but there was the messianic "age to come" (Eph 1:21, Heb 6:4). When Messiah came, he would usher in a new covenant, a new age of spiritual transformation in the world.

Well, of course, Messiah had come. That "age to come" was not a reference to a second coming of Jesus, but his first coming, bringing the kingdom of God (the kingdom age to come), a kingdom that was both now and not yet. It was inaugurated but not consummated.

This "age to come" was the new covenant age. Paul wrote elsewhere that the gospel (the new covenant) was "hidden for ages, <u>but now revealed</u> to his saints (Col 1:26). In 1 Corinthians 10:11, he wrote that the old covenant events occurred as an example "for our instruction <u>upon whom the end of the ages has come</u>." Did you catch that? The temple had not yet been destroyed, and Paul was saying that his generation was at the end of the ages! He said that it *had come* upon that first century of believers. The end of the age is not

---

[1] Johannes P. Louw and Eugene Albert Nida, *Greek-English Lexicon of the New Testament: Based on Semantic Domains* (New York: United Bible Societies, 1996), 647.

a future event that hasn't happened yet; it occurred in the first century with the coming of the new covenant, confirmed in the destruction of the temple. But Paul isn't the only one who wrote that in the New Testament.

Hebrews 9:26 says that Jesus suffered on the cross, "once for all at the end of the ages to put away sin by the sacrifice of himself." The end of the ages is not the end of history or the end of the world as we understand it. The end of the ages had already occurred at the time of the crucifixion of Christ. The end of the ages was the end of the old covenant era and the beginning of the new covenant in Christ's blood!

But get this: that same writer of Hebrews talked about the new covenant in Christ being superior to the old covenant in Hebrews 8. He quoted Jeremiah confirming that the prophets predicted the arrival of the new covenant age. And then he said, "In speaking of a new covenant, he makes the first one obsolete. And what is becoming obsolete and growing old is ready to vanish away" (8:13).

What was growing old and ready to vanish at that time?

It blew my theology when I realized that he was talking about the destruction of the temple as the final culmination of the new covenant replacement of the old covenant! He was writing in the time period after Christ's death and resurrection and right before the temple had been destroyed. So the new covenant had been established in Christ's blood, but it was not consummated with historical finality. Like Paul, the writer believed they were at the end of the ages. The new covenant would make the old covenant obsolete. But take a closer look at the language he used. He said that the old is "becoming obsolete and is ready to vanish away," as if the old covenant had not vanished yet. It was only in the process of *becoming* obsolete. "Becoming," not "had become," and not "would become" thousands of years in the future. What could that mean?

Well, the writer was writing within the generation that Jesus said would see the destruction of the temple. The temple had not yet been destroyed. Hebrews 8 says that they were in a time period of change between covenants and that change had not yet been fully or historically consummated. That first century generation was in the transition period between ages or covenants. So, what would be the event that would embody the theological claim that the old covenant was obsolete and the new covenant had replaced it? The destruction of the symbol of the old covenant, the temple! The old covenant would not be obsolete until its symbolic incarnation, the temple, was made desolate.[2]

I had to eventually admit that the "end of the ages" did not mean what I was taught it meant, or what we modern Westerners assume it means. It did not mean the end of history, or the second coming of Christ, but, rather, to the New Testament writers, it meant the end of God's old covenant age.

Latter Days

This brings me to the other term that is so often misinterpreted by Christians as a reference to the end of history: "the last days." You hear a lot from Christians proclaiming we are in the last days. Quite frankly, its cult-like the way some obsess over it. They start to sound more excited to see God's judgment than they do to see the growth of his kingdom. I too had thought that the last days were the last days of history before the rise of the Antichrist and the great tribulation that would lead to the return of Christ. I mean, what else could they be? Wasn't it spelled out explicitly all over the prophecies of the Bible?

I would soon discover that, yet again, my modern Western mind, untutored in the worldview of ancient Jews of the Old Testament, simply misinterpreted that concept for lack of knowledge.

First of all, the term *last days* is derived from the Old Testament term *latter days*, that shows up quite a bit. On the surface to us, the term *latter days* may sound like a prophetic hint at the last days of history, but it really only means "many years from now" in a generic sense. Latter days is not the name of a specific time period in history, but rather it is applied to many different periods throughout old covenant history.

Let's take a brief look at just a few of them.

In Genesis 49:1, Jacob called together his twelve sons and told them, "Gather yourselves together, that I may tell you what shall happen to you in

---

[2] In an interesting passage of *Wars of the Jews*, Josephus describes the destruction of the temple in A.D. 70 as being a fulfillment of a prophecy most likely from Daniel about the abomination of desolation, the very prophecy Jesus warned about in Matthew 24:15! "for there was a certain ancient oracle of those men, that the city should then be taken and the sanctuary burnt, by right of war, when a sedition should invade the Jews, and their own hand should pollute the temple of God." Flavius Josephus and William Whiston, *The Works of Josephus: Complete and Unabridged* (Peabody: Hendrickson, 1987) *Wars*, 4.388.

the latter days." The events that Jacob then prophesied occurred during the time of Old Testament history, not in some end of the world.

In Deuteronomy 31:29, Moses told the people of Israel as they were about to enter the Promised Land, "After my death you will surely act corruptly and turn aside from the way that I have commanded you. And in the latter days evil will befall you, because you will do what is evil in the sight of the Lord." The Old Testament is a virtual history lesson of fulfillment of this prophecy. In fact, God said this prophecy of latter days was fulfilled in the time of the book of Judges when he said, "Because this people have transgressed my covenant that I commanded their fathers and have not obeyed my voice, I will no longer drive out before them any of the nations" (Judges 2:20). The latter days for Moses meant "in the days to come" not "at the end of history," and they were fulfilled in Old Testament history.

In Daniel 2:28, Daniel prepared to explain to King Nebuchadnezzar his mysterious dream. He said that God "has made known to King Nebuchadnezzar what will be in the latter days." He then described the statue that symbolized the four successive kingdoms beginning with Nebuchadnezzar's Babylon and moving to Medo-Persia, Greece, and Rome. The latter days for Daniel were fulfilled in his own lifetime and up to the rise of ancient Rome. Daniel's latter days are thousands of years in our past, not thousands of years in his future.

There are many other examples in the Old Testament of this phrase "latter days" being used as a generic term to mean "in the days to come."[3]

---

[3] The following chart is from Gary DeMar, *Why the End of the World is Not in Your Future*, (Georgia, American Vision Press, 2010), 91.

In the Latter Days	**Fulfillment**
Genesis 49:1	Jacob's immediate descendants
Numbers 24:14	David crushed the Moabites
Deuteronomy 4:30	Period of the Judges
Deuteronomy 31:29	Period of the Judges and following
Isaiah 2:2-4; Micah 4:1	Period of the Messiah
Jeremiah 23:30; 30:24	Babylon
Jeremiah 48:47	Pentecost
Jeremiah 49:39	Pentecost
Daniel 2:28	Succession of world powers
Daniel 8:17,19	Antiochus Epiphanes (175-164 B.C.)
Daniel 10:14	Cyrus to Antiochus
Hosea 3:5	Acts 2

"Latter days" seems to us to be the title of the last days of history only because of our bias; however, they were actually fulfilled in our past.

But what about the few scriptures that seem to use "latter days" in reference to the second coming of Christ? What about their connection to the New Testament equivalent phrase "last days"?

Get ready for another surprise.

The Last Days

There are several Old Testament passages that, to our Western eyes, appear to refer to the second coming of Christ (Isaiah 2:2-4; Micah 4:1; Joel 2:28-32). In these passages the last days do speak of the coming of Messiah; but they do not link those days with the *second* coming of Messiah, but, rather, the *first* coming.

> Isaiah 2:2–4 (NASB95)
> Now it will come about that In the last days The mountain of the house of the LORD Will be established as the chief of the mountains, And will be raised above the hills; And all the nations will stream to it. [3] And many peoples will come and say, "Come, let us go up to the mountain of the LORD, To the house of the God of Jacob; That He may teach us concerning His ways And that we may walk in His paths." For the law will go forth from Zion And the word of the LORD from Jerusalem. [4] And He will judge between the nations, And will render decisions for many peoples; And they will hammer their swords into plowshares and their spears into pruning hooks. Nation will not lift up sword against nation, And never again will they learn war.

The reason why I originally thought this was a reference to the physical return of Christ was because of how the verses ended: "He will judge between the nations…and never again will they learn of war." How could this possibly be a reference to anything other than the end of history? All nations are not streaming into the kingdom of God yet, are they?

Well, according to the New Testament, the conversion of people from all nations (streaming to God's kingdom) is exactly what the gospel started to achieve in the first century. Paul wrote in Romans that even in his lifetime, the gospel "has been made known to all nations…to bring about the obedience of faith" (Rom 16:25-26). The picture of the nations streaming to the mountain of the house of the Lord is an image of people from every nation becoming Christians (1 Tim 3:16). Remember the cornerstone of Jesus the Messiah that crushed the feet of Nebuchadnezzar's dream statue? According to the prophecy, the coming of Messiah in the first century brought about the ultimate fall of Rome and the establishment of God's kingdom that would grow to be a mountain that filled the earth.

> Daniel 2:35, 44
> But the stone that struck the image became a great mountain and filled the whole earth… [44] And in the days of those kings the God of heaven will set up a kingdom that shall never be destroyed, nor shall the kingdom be left to another people. It shall break in pieces all these kingdoms and bring them to an end, and it shall stand forever.

That mountain in Daniel is the mountain of the kingdom of God established by the first coming of Jesus Christ. It is the same "mountain of the house of the Lord" in Isaiah 2. Of course, it has to take time to grow to fill the earth, and that is what the kingdom of God does throughout history. The leaven of God's kingdom takes time to fill all the dough; the mustard seed takes time to grow before it is the biggest tree in the garden (Matt 13:31-33). But it began with Jesus in the first century at his first coming. God set up his kingdom "in the days of those kings," ending with Rome of the first century.

So in Isaiah 2, the last days were the last days of the old covenant that began with Messiah Jesus establishing the mountain at his first coming. But then that mountain would begin to grow to fill the earth with the conversion of Christians, and, one day in our distant future, wars will cease. But the mountain of the new covenant was established in the last days of the old covenant in the first century.

So the last days prophecy of Isaiah 2 (and Daniel 2) is a prophecy about the end of the old covenant and the beginning of the new covenant. But that prophecy paints a picture of what the kingdom of God eventually accomplishes. The last days in Isaiah and Micah are not the last days of history but the last days of the old covenant in the first century that heralded the beginning of a new covenant that will lead to a new end in history. Just give it some time. It's been inaugurated but not consummated. In other words, it's already, but not yet.

But don't take my word for it. The New Testament writers explained over and over again that the last days were in the first century—in our past, not our future. For those who claim to be literalists, it is crystal clear that the writers of the New Testament called their own days the last days, the last times, even, the last hour, which are all expressions of the urgency of their own day, not some day thousands of years later. Look at these verses.

> Hebrews 1:1–2 (written in the first century)
> Long ago, at many times and in many ways, God spoke to our fathers by the prophets, [2] but in these last days he has spoken to us by his Son.
>
> 1 Peter 1:20 (written in the first century)
> He was foreknown before the foundation of the world but was made manifest in the last times for the sake of you.
>
> 1 John 2:18 (written in the first century)
> Children, it is the last hour, and as you have heard that antichrist is coming, so now many antichrists have come. Therefore we know that it is the last hour.
>
> 1 Peter 4:7 (written in the first century)
> The end of all things is at hand; therefore be self-controlled and sober-minded for the sake of your prayers.
>
> 1 Corinthians 10:11 (written in the first century)
> Now these things happened to them as an example, but they were written down for our instruction, on whom the end of the ages has come.

Jude and Paul wrote about the prophecies of the last days describing the kind of evil that would occur (Jude 17-19; 2 Tim 3:1-8). I had read these with my assumptions that they were talking about the distant future, in other words, *my days*, not their days. But that was only because I was taught to assume that these things had not happened yet. When I read them more closely in context, I could see that the apostolic authors were talking about such evil occurring *in their own day*. They were saying those prophecies had come true in the wickedness they themselves were experiencing, not in some distant future thousands of years from then.

The final nail in the coffin of the last days madness that I had been caught up in was in Acts 2.

In Acts 2, Peter was preaching on the day of Pentecost. Jews from many nations had been filled with the Spirit of God and began to speak gospel truth in their own tongues. The nations were beginning to stream into the mountain of the house of the Lord, the new covenant. Unbelievers accused them of being drunk and Peter responded.

> Acts 2:15–20
> For these people are not drunk, as you suppose, since it is only the third hour of the day. [16] But this is what was uttered through the prophet Joel: [17] "And in the last days it shall be, God declares, that I will pour out my Spirit on all flesh, and your sons and your daughters shall prophesy, and your young men shall see visions, and your old men shall dream dreams; [18] even on my male servants and female servants in those days I will pour out my Spirit, and they shall prophesy. [19] And I will show wonders in the heavens above and signs on the earth below, blood, and fire, and vapor of smoke; [20] the sun shall be turned to darkness and the moon to blood, before the day of the Lord comes, the great and magnificent day."

Look at what I underlined. Peter said that the Spirit of God falling on "all flesh" at Pentecost (another figurative, nonliteral expression for Gentiles and the nations outside of Israel) was the fulfillment of Joel's prophecy about the last days!

That had always bothered me because I wondered how he could say that the last days were his own days when the day of the Lord was not for another few thousand years? What about the sun and moon turning dark? Was that all just a metaphor, or did he literally mean what he said?

He was an apostle who spoke with God's authority and he said that the last days prophecy was being fulfilled in his own day, not thousands of years later. We have already discussed the notion that in the Old Testament the cosmic catastrophes of sun, moon, and stars were poetic metaphors for the fall of earthly and spiritual powers. And we also learned that the day of the Lord was not necessarily the end of history but a day of judgment on a nation or people or city.

And the temple and Jerusalem had not yet been destroyed as Jesus predicted. So the Spirit of God being poured out on the nations began to be fulfilled at Pentecost, and that happened just years before the heavenly and earthly power of Israel was abolished in the destruction of the holy city and temple. The last days were the last days of the old covenant that was replaced by the new covenant mountain of God, finalized in the destruction of the Jewish temple and holy city.

Okay, so two out of the three things that the disciples asked Jesus about were to take place in the first century: the destruction of the temple and city, which marked the end of the age or last days of the old covenant. But what about the third question, the "sign of Christ's coming"? It seemed pretty certain *that* event could not have taken place in the first century. So maybe there is a division between these three things. Maybe Jesus prophesied the destruction of the temple in A.D. 70 but then he jumped ahead thousands of years to his physical return, just like Daniel and Isaiah did. By starting with the inauguration of the last days, he envisioned the end of that beginning by jumping to the end of history where the mountain has filled the earth and there is no longer any war.

Fair enough. But the prophecy of his coming doesn't occur until Matthew 24:27. Before that event, Jesus described a series of birth pains that would lead up to his coming. So let's first take a look at those.

Chapter 10
Birth Pains

Jesus' disciples asked him when the destruction of the temple would occur—the event that marked the end of the age of the old covenant—and when would be the sign of his coming. Jesus responded by giving a list of predictions of the near future. I had always been troubled by those predictions because they seemed so generic that you could apply them to just about any age. But when I studied the time period of the generation of Jesus, I uncovered some amazing facts that confirmed their fulfillment in that first century.

I will address these under the following categories in the rough order that Jesus mentioned them: (1) false prophets and christs, (2) great tribulation (3) wars and rumors of wars, (4) famines and earthquakes, (5) the gospel proclaimed to the world, and (6) the abomination of desolation.

"You," Not "They"

Before I embark on my medical-theological examination of the birth pains, I want to remind you of the context of all the statements throughout the discourse. When Christians read the prophecy, they tend to assume that Jesus was referring to a distant generation, thousands of years later. So therefore, they read his statements as if he is speaking to us or our near-future brethren in Christ. But remember, when he said, "this generation" (Matt 23:36; 24:34), it meant the first century generation he was speaking to. It was *this generation* that was guilty of murdering Christ; it was *this generation* who would see and experience the destruction of God's house (23:38).

So when Jesus said, "Woe to you scribes and Pharisees" (23:29), he meant the scribes and Pharisees who were listening to his sermon, not a future generation of scribes and Pharisees. When he said, "You see all these" buildings and temples (24:2), he was talking to his disciples, not a distant generation of disciples. His entire discourse contains over forty references to "you"—forty! If literalists pride themselves on taking prophecies literally, they must be quite uncomfortable when they have to twist the obvious, literal referents of Jesus' words to be figuratively applied to someone else thousands of years later.

Consider these statements in Matthew. The italics are mine. Jesus said to his listeners, "Truly, I say to *you*" (23:36), "For I tell *you*" (23:39), "Truly, I say to *you*" (24:2), "If anyone says to *you*" (24:23), "when *you* see all these things" (24:33), "See, I have told *you*" (24:25), "Truly, I say to *you*" (24:34), "Therefore *you* also must be ready" (24:44), "Truly I say to *you*" (24:47). That alone should cause futurists to pause. Imagine how confused the disciples would be thinking that Jesus was talking to them when he really meant someone else.

Truly, I say to *you*, dear reader of this book, imagine sitting in a sermon at church where a pastor keeps speaking to you but he does not mean you, but rather another future generation of Christians. You would certainly look around and think to yourself, Why is he saying "you" as if he is speaking to us? Why isn't he saying "they?"

So the context of the entire discourse is speaking to those who were listening to him: *you*, not *they*.

False Prophets and False Christs

Jesus predicted the coming of false prophets and false christs several times throughout his discourse.

> Matthew 24:4–5
> See that no one leads you astray. [5] For many will come in my name, saying, "I am the Christ," and they will lead many astray.
>
> Matthew 24:11–13
> And many false prophets will arise and lead many astray. [12] And because lawlessness will be increased, the love of many will grow cold. [13] But the one who endures to the end will be saved.
>
> Matthew 24:23–26
> Then if anyone says to you, "Look, here is the Christ!" or "There he is!" do not believe it. [24] For false christs and false prophets will arise and perform great signs and wonders, so as to lead astray, if possible, even the elect. [25] See, I have

> told you beforehand. [26] So, if they say to you, "Look, he is in the wilderness," do not go out. If they say, "Look, he is in the inner rooms," do not believe it.

Now, of course, there have been false prophets and false christs through all of history. So how could this be of much help? Think about it; when would a prophecy of false christs be most relevant? The answer is in Jesus' own words when he compared the claims of such imposters with the real coming of the Son of Man in 24:27. The relevance of false christs is when Christ does come; it will not be as a man in the wilderness, but it will be swift and powerful like the lightning that cracks the sky with ferocity (24:27). I will discuss the actual coming of Christ, called the *parousia*, in a later chapter. Right now, I just want to make the point that his coming in this verse is not *in the sky* like lightning, but merely *swift and powerful* like lightning. The analogy is one of high impact versus low impact, not of earth versus sky.

Anyone who has read the entire New Testament knows that there are many references to false prophets and false christs throughout the early church that fit this prophecy. In fact, it seems that much of the New Testament was written in response to false prophets and teachers deceiving the elect, if that were possible. Here is a listing of some of them.

Acts 5:36-37	Theudas and Judas of Galilee
Acts 8:9-10	Simon the magician
Acts 13:6	Bar-Jesus the false prophet
Acts 20:29-30	false prophets in Ephesus after Paul left them
2 Timothy 1:15	Phygelus and Hermogenes false teachers
2 Timothy 3:1-13	False prophets and teachers
2 Corinthians 11:12-15	False apostles
Galatians 1:4-6	False brethren
Revelation 2:14-15	The Nicolaitans, false teaching
Revelation 2:20-24	Jezebel, false teaching lead astray
2 Peter 2:1	False prophets/false teachers through Dispersion
1 John 2:18-26	Many antichrists false teaching
1 John 4:1-3	"Many" false prophets, antichrists in the first century world
2 John 7-9	Deceivers, antichrists

Since most Jews did not believe in Jesus, they were still looking for Messiah because Daniel's prophecy had told them he would appear around the time of their generation. So the time was unique for Jewish false christs in a way that it would not be for the rest of history. Jesus' prophecy about false prophets and false christs was being fulfilled at the time of the birth of the early church before A.D. 70.

But there is another element of this prophecy that roots it in the first century context for fulfillment. Why would Jesus talk about false messiahs *being in the wilderness*? That doesn't sound too modern in a world where false prophets in the cities have far more impact than some secret, suicidal sect or survivalist camp. But in the ancient world around Jerusalem, the wilderness was very relevant. The Jewish historian Josephus provided us with the answer. He wrote about the Jewish revolt that began around A.D. 66 that lead to the destruction of the temple in A.D. 70. And in that time period he explained how the non-christian Jews were looking for the Christ to rise up and lead them in military victory against the Romans. Many revolutionaries, such as the Zealots, followed leaders who tried to gather forces around themselves as the promised messiah. And guess where many of them hid out and did their dirty deeds? You guessed it— in the wilderness of Israel.

Here are a couple of the many passages from Josephus that give us a flavor of the fulfillment of Jesus' predictions about false messiahs in the wilderness. The underlining is mine.

> Now it came to pass, while Fadus was procurator of Judea, that a certain magician, whose name was Theudas, [the same Theudas spoken of in Acts 5:36-37] persuaded a great part of the people to take their effects with them, and follow him to the river Jordan; for he told them he was a prophet, and that he would, by his own command, divide the river, and afford them an easy passage over it; and many were deluded by his words. However, Fadus did not permit them to make any advantage of his wild attempt, but sent a troop of horsemen out against them; who, falling upon them unexpectedly, slew many of them and took many of them alive. They also took Theudas alive, and cut off his head, and carried it to Jerusalem.[1]

---

[1] Flavius Josephus and William Whiston, *The Works of Josephus: Complete and Unabridged* (Peabody: Hendrickson, 1987). *Antiquities* 20.97–98.

> There was also another body of wicked men gotten together, not so impure in their actions, but more wicked in their intentions, who laid waste the happy state of the city no less than did these murderers. These were such men as deceived and deluded the people under pretense of divine inspiration, but were for procuring innovations and changes of the government, and these prevailed with the multitude to act like madmen, and went before them into the wilderness, as pretending that God would there show them the signals of liberty…
>
> But there was an Egyptian false prophet that did the Jews more mischief than the former; for he was a cheat, and pretended to be a prophet also, and got together thirty thousand men that were deluded by him; these he led round about from the wilderness to the mount which was called the Mount of Olives, and was ready to break into Jerusalem by force from that place; and if he could but once conquer the Roman garrison and the people, he intended to domineer over them by the assistance of those guards of his that were to break into the city with him.[2]

The fulfillment of false prophets and false messiahs has particular relevance to the first century that led up to the destruction of the temple in A.D. 70. Messianic fever was highest in this very time period. But that is not all. The persecution of the original disciples was also an important part of Jesus' prophecy.

Great Tribulation

Persecution of Christianity is nothing new to history. In fact, in terms of sheer numbers, we have more Christians being persecuted now for the faith than in all of history. But it's not about the literal numbers; it's about the end of the age. And remember "the end" is the end of the Old Testament age.

---

[2] Flavius Josephus and William Whiston, *The Works of Josephus: Complete and Unabridged* (Peabody: Hendrickson, 1987). *Wars of the Jews*, 2.258-263.

> Matthew 24:9–13
> Then they will deliver you up to tribulation and put you to death, and you will be hated by all nations for my name's sake. [10] And then many will fall away and betray one another and hate one another...[12] And because lawlessness will be increased, the love of many will grow cold. [13] But the one who endures to the end will be saved.

Luke's version of this same prophecy adds more detail and context.

> Luke 21:12–19
> But before all this they will lay their hands on you and persecute you, delivering you up to the synagogues and prisons, and you will be brought before kings and governors for my name's sake. [13] This will be your opportunity to bear witness. [14] Settle it therefore in your minds not to meditate beforehand how to answer, [15] for I will give you a mouth and wisdom, which none of your adversaries will be able to withstand or contradict. [16] You will be delivered up even by parents and brothers and relatives and friends, and some of you they will put to death. [17] You will be hated by all for my name's sake. [18] But not a hair of your head will perish. [19] By your endurance you will gain your lives.

Within a few short years of this prophecy, "a great persecution arose against the church in Jerusalem; and they were all scattered throughout the regions of Judea and Samaria" (Acts 8:1). The disciples were brought before kings and governors, just as Jesus said they would be (Acts 25:6-26:1; 2 Cor 11:24-26).

Within a generation after the Jews persecuted the Christians, the Roman empire joined in. We know from history that Nero began his persecution of Christians throughout the empire around A.D. 64.[3] But the apostles endured

---

[3] Tacitus, *Annals* 15:44+: "Therefore, to scotch the rumour, Nero substituted as culprits, and punished with the utmost refinements of cruelty, a class of men, loathed for their vices, whom the crowd styled Christians. Christus, the founder of the name, had undergone the death penalty in the reign of Tiberius, by sentence of the procurator Pontius Pilatus, and the pernicious superstition was checked for a moment, only to break out once more, not merely in Judaea, the home of the disease, but in the capital itself, where

to the end. They were not saved from death (since Jesus clearly said some would die); but they were saved from the judgment of God because they endured in their faith and in the gospel. (For a fictional narrative of these events see my Chronicles of the Apocalypse.)

Just How Great Is It?

One of the terms used by futurists of this persecution and tribulation is "the great tribulation," based on Jesus' own designation in Matthew 24:21. According to futurists it is supposed to be a seven year period under the Antichrist in our future. This tribulation is supposed to be so great and worldwide that it will be unparalleled in history. It will consist not only of geopolitical events and wars but of persecution and suffering under the judgments of God.

But Jesus added something that throws another wrench into the typical futurist paradigm of the end of the world—that old wrench of hyperbole.

> Matthew 24:21
> For then there will be great tribulation, such as has not been from the beginning of the world until now, no, and never will be.

When I first studied this, it seemed obvious to me that the great tribulation had not occurred yet, since we have not seen a time period of persecution that "has not been from the beginning of the world, until now, no and never will be." As Lindsey and *Left Behind* taught me, that would have to be so horrendous that nothing could top it.

However, as I studied the language more closely, I discovered that this kind of hyperbole was common, not just in Hebrew writing but in the Bible. In fact, literalists would find themselves with a biblical contradiction if they did not acknowledge the poetic exaggeration. Here's why.

---

all things horrible or shameful in the world collect and find a vogue. First, then, the confessed members of the sect were arrested; next, on their disclosures, vast numbers were convicted, not so much on the count of arson as for hatred of the human race. And derision accompanied their end: they were covered with wild beasts' skins and torn to death by dogs; or they were fastened on crosses, and, when daylight failed were burned to serve as lamps by night. Nero had offered his Gardens for the spectacle, and gave an exhibition in his Circus, mixing with the crowd in the habit of a charioteer, or mounted on his car. Hence, in spite of a guilt which had earned the most exemplary punishment, there arose a sentiment of pity, due to the impression that they were being sacrificed not for the welfare of the state but to the ferocity of a single man."

In 587-586 B.C., Babylon invaded Israel, besieged Jerusalem, destroyed the temple, and exiled most of the Jews in a great dispersion or Diaspora. Ezekiel gave us God's own words of the event.

> Ezekiel 5:9
> And because of all your abominations I will do with you what I have never yet done, and the like of which I will never do again.

Daniel echoed these same words of the Babylonian exile.

> Daniel 9:12
> He has confirmed his words, which he spoke against us and against our rulers who ruled us, by bringing upon us a great calamity. <u>For under the whole heaven there has not been done anything like what has been done against Jerusalem</u>.

So both Daniel and Ezekiel used the same exact language that Jesus used: "There has not been done anything like it" and "never again" will it be done. And they were both talking about a foreign enemy destroying Jerusalem.

Yet in A.D. 70, the Romans did exactly the same thing as the Babylonians. They were foreigners who besieged Jerusalem, destroyed the temple and city, and carried away the Jews into exile. And God orchestrated both times for the same reason: the rulers of Israel had led the people into corruption. God did the exact same thing at least two times.

Now at this point, I don't see how anyone can maintain a commitment to a wooden, literalist interpretation of the great tribulation as being unequaled. You either have to claim the Bible contradicts itself or you have to admit the phrase "never been done and never will be done" is poetic hyperbole that is used multiple times—whenever there is massive destruction.

But I'm not finished. Remember that passage I addressed earlier in Joel 2 about the last days? Remember that Peter said that the passage about the last days was being fulfilled right before their eyes, beginning at Pentecost of the first century? Well, guess what, he also added this "never like it" phrase as well.

> Joel 2:1–2 (NASB95)
> For the day of the LORD is coming; Surely it is near, [2] A day of darkness and gloom, A day of clouds and thick darkness.

> As the dawn is spread over the mountains, *So* there is a great and mighty people; There has never been *anything* like it, Nor will there be again after it To the years of many generations.

So the day of the Lord in Joel that was coming in the last days of the first century consisted of a mighty people (the Romans), who, exactly like the Babylonians, would besiege Jerusalem, destroy the temple, and carry them away into exile. Yet, Joel said and Peter affirmed, "There has never been anything like it, nor will there be again after it."

This can only be described as hyperbole, or the Bible believer suffers under the weight of biblical contradiction created by their own eschatological system.

And speaking of hyperbole, if the futurist thinks that the great tribulation is literally unequalled, then they have another contradiction to consider. The flood of Noah's day that killed every single person on the land except eight people was surely the greatest of all tribulations and destruction unequalled in all of history (1 Pet 3:20). It was surely greater than the Babylonian destruction and exile of Israel, and even greater than the worst futurist Antichrist scenario they imagine. Yet this can only be true if the phrase "never had been nor will be" is poetic license used of any event that is massive in its devastation.

There is still another problem with the futurist scenario of the tribulation. The apostle John wrote the book of Revelation in the first century, and look at what he wrote of the tribulation.

> Revelation 1:9
> I, John, your brother and partner in the tribulation and the kingdom and the patient endurance that are in Jesus.

What? The tribulation was going on in the first century while the apostle John was still alive? John then wrote in Revelation about that "hour of testing which is about to come upon the whole world, to test those who dwell upon the earth" (Rev 3:10). As everyone knows, the book of Revelation is about those end times events. So for him to say the tribulation was already going on is yet another strong indicator that those end times events were already occurring in the first century.

And Peter concurred with John when he wrote to the persecuted Christians who lived around A.D. 60 that they should endure because "the end of all things is at hand" (1 Pet 4:7). This "end" was the same end of the old covenant age that was yet to conclude when he penned that letter. The "end of all things" was not the end of the space-time universe or the end of history; it was the end of the old covenant embodied in the temple system.

The tribulation was occurring in the first century. The end was near.

Wars and Rumors of Wars

The next thing Jesus predicted was wars and rumors of wars.

> Matthew 24:6–7
> And you will hear of wars and rumors of wars. See that you are not alarmed, for this must take place, but the end is not yet. [7] For nation will rise against nation, and kingdom against kingdom.

This had always been one of the more troubling predictions to me when I thought we were on the verge of the rapture in my lifetime. Why? Because this is another one of those prophecies that is so generic it could be applied to any time period of history. Is that really a prophecy? If I said to you that Jesus was coming soon because look at how there are so many wars and rumors of wars around us, you would laugh at me. This is no different than any other time period in history.

Except one: the first century time period of *Pax Romana.*

When I found out more about the Roman empire of that time period, this prophecy began to stand out with a sharper clarity. The term *Pax Romana* is Latin for "the peace of Rome." By the time of Augustus in 27 B.C., just before Christ, Rome had conquered the known world of that time and therefore had subjugated all the warring nations under its authority. This effectively stopped wars and ushered in an unprecedented time of peace. Yes, imperial peace, which would not to our modern understanding appear to be very just or peaceful. But in their eyes it would be. It was in this context of the peace of Rome that the New Testament prophecy of wars and rumors of wars would make more sense than during our own time period. This was also the time of the Jewish uprising that led to war as well.

A famous Roman historian wrote of this time period, about A.D. 69, where *Pax Romana* broke down in fulfillment of Jesus' words.

> Tacitus, *Histories* 1.2
> (January - March, A.D. 69) The history on which I am entering is that of a period rich in disasters, terrible with battles, torn by civil struggles, horrible even in peace. Four emperors fell by the sword; there were three civil wars, more foreign wars, and often both at the same time. There was success in the East, misfortune in the West. Illyricum was disturbed, the Gallic provinces wavering, Britain subdued and immediately let go. The Sarmatae and Suebi rose against us; the Dacians won fame by defeats inflicted and suffered; even the Parthians were almost roused to arms through the trickery of a pretended Nero. Moreover, Italy was distressed by disasters unknown before or returning after the lapse of ages. Cities on the rich fertile shores of Campania were swallowed up or overwhelmed; Rome was devastated by conflagrations, in which her most ancient shrines were consumed and the very Capitol fired by citizens' hands. Sacred rites were defiled; there were adulteries in high places. The sea was filled with exiles, its cliffs made foul with the bodies of the dead.[4]

Wars and rumors of wars indeed!

Famines and Earthquakes

> Matthew 24:7
> And there will be famines and earthquakes in various places.

Okay, maybe wars and rumors of wars weren't the most generic after all. Famines and earthquakes in various places? I had thought, How generic can you get, Jesus? You sure are making it hard to prove your prophecies are actually prophecies.

---

[4] http://penelope.uchicago.edu/Thayer/E/Roman/Texts/Tacitus/Histories/1A*.html

Well, one of the constant "proofs" that many futurists try to point to for their interpretation is the increase in frequency of earthquakes as one of the signs of the coming of Christ in our time. I bought that at first, but the more I looked into it, the less weight it carried in convincing me. Jesus didn't say there would be an increase in earthquakes; he said there would be famines and earthquakes *in various places*. To add the concept of increase of magnitude or number of earthquakes to that prophecy is a sleight of hand, twisting the context to fit a preconceived scheme. It is adding to the Word of God. And it is certainly not literal.

And then I found out that the very claim of increased earthquakes in our era was simply factually false.[5] We have advanced technology and worldwide connections that allow us to record far more tremors than ever in history. That is an increase in measuring sensitivity, not an increase in activity. The facts don't even fit the rattling interpretation.

What about famines? The New Testament speaks of "a great famine all over the world" that took place in the reign of emperor Claudius (Acts 11:27-29). Josephus wrote of famines and earthquakes, especially near the time period of A.D. 70 (*Wars of the Jews* 6.299-300; 1.370-371; 4.286-287; 5.25-26; 6.193-200).

Tacitus wrote of famines and earthquakes in the Roman empire.

> This year witnessed many prodigies [signs and omens].... repeated earthquakes... further portents were seen in a shortage of corn, resulting in famine... It was established that there was no more than fifteen days supply of food in the city [Rome]. Only Heaven's special favour and a mild winter prevented catastrophe.[6]

Seneca, who lived in the first century, also wrote of the massive earthquakes in various places.

> How often have cities in Asia, how often in Achaia, been laid low by a single shock of earthquake! How many towns

---

[5] Steven A. Austin and Mark L. Strauss, "Are Earthquakes Signs of the End Times?" Christian Research Institute website, http://www.equip.org/article/are-earthquakes-signs-of-the-end-times/

[6] Tacitus, *The Annals*, 12.43, Michael Grant, (Penguin Books 1989), page 271.

> in Syria, how many in Macedonia, have been swallowed up! How often has this kind of devastation laid Cyprus in ruins! How often had Paphos collapsed! Not infrequently are tidings brought to us of the utter destruction of entire cities.[7]

In the ancient Roman empire of the first century, such earthquakes in various places were strong indicators of coming judgment.

Gospel Proclaimed to the World

At this point in Jesus' discourse, he predicted the worldwide proclamation of the gospel before the end.

> Matthew 24:14
> And this gospel of the kingdom will be proclaimed throughout the whole world as a testimony to all nations, and then the end will come.

When I was a futurist, I used to cling to this verse as an assurance that these prophecies could not have possibly occurred in the past because the gospel had *obviously* not been preached to the whole world yet. In fact, I believed that it was only with the advent of modern technology that we now had the actual ability to even fulfill that prediction of world missions. Even now, there are still stone age tribes in obscure jungles of the world that have not yet heard the gospel of Jesus Christ. No, I thought, surely the Olivet Discourse prophecies had to be in our future because the gospel had not been proclaimed throughout the whole world to all the nations as Jesus predicted.

And then I discovered that the Bible said it had been.

First of all, the Greek word that is used for "whole world" is *oikoumene*, which is an ancient idiom that referred to the Roman empire. As we already learned in the chapter on describing what "all the nations" meant, it was common for empires like Babylon and Rome to praise themselves with the hyperbole of being rulers over "all peoples, nations, and languages that dwell on the earth" (Dan 4:1). They claimed that they owned "all the kingdoms of

---

[7] Seneca in "Seneca Ad Lucilium Epistulae Morales," Translated by Richard M Gummere, Vol 2, pg 437.

the earth" (Ezra 1:1) when, in fact, they did not rule over any countries on the other side of the earth. But to them, their kingdoms were "the whole world."

Thus it is no surprise when Luke used that same word, *oikoumene*, when he wrote that in the days of Caesar Augustus, a census was taken "of all the world" (Luke 2:1). The census was taken of the Roman empire, not the whole world as we now understand that term. The whole world meant the Roman empire to them. Later Luke also spoke of a famine that took place "over all the world" (Acts 11:28), which was a reference to a famine in the Roman empire. "All the world," simply meant all over the empire.

Again, hyperbole is so frequently a part of Hebrew thought that it is no wonder that hyperliteralists come up with bizarre interpretations of prophecy because they ignore the poetic dimension. Jesus didn't mean that the end would not come until every single person or even tribe or nation had a chance to hear the gospel, as popular prophecy pundits proclaim. He meant that the gospel would spread throughout the entire Roman empire before the end of the old covenant age was fully over in the destruction of the holy temple.

But again, don't take my word for it. The apostle Paul stated over and over again that this gospel prophecy had been fulfilled in his lifetime; so the end of the ages was upon them in the first century.

Paul used the same hyperbole as Jesus when he wrote that the gospel "was proclaimed in all creation under heaven" during his own ministry.

> Colossians 1:23
> The hope of the gospel that you heard, which has been proclaimed in all creation under heaven, and of which I, Paul, became a minister.

"All creation under heaven" is certainly an even broader scope than "all the nations," or "the whole world." And he was certainly not saying that the gospel was preached in the American continent (which wasn't named America at the time because nobody there knew it even existed).

In Romans 16: 25-26, Paul talked about the mystery of the gospel

> that was kept secret for long ages [26] but has now been disclosed and through the prophetic writings has been made known to all nations, according to the command of the eternal God, to bring about the obedience of faith.

According to Paul, the gospel had been made known to all nations. Paul wrote to Timothy explaining that this mysterious gospel was contained in doctrinal truths.

> 1 Timothy 3:16
> [Jesus] was manifested in the flesh, vindicated by the Spirit, seen by angels, proclaimed among the nations, believed on in the world, taken up in glory.

The major author of the New Testament wrote that Jesus' prophecy about the gospel being proclaimed to all the world and all the nations was already fulfilled in his lifetime and that the end was therefore near in the first century, not in some distant future thousands of years later.

If the Bible itself says that a prophecy is fulfilled, who are we to say it has not been fulfilled? Do we reinterpret the Bible to fit our theology or do we change our theology to fit the Bible?

So, as we've walked through the birth pains that Jesus predicted before his coming and the end of the age, we have seen that the end of the age was the end of the old covenant age embodied in the temple system and that the last days were the last days of that old covenant system that was replaced by the new covenant in the first century. We saw that Jesus was talking to his contemporaries, not some distant, future generation and that the prophecies of false prophets, false christs, great tribulation, wars and rumors of wars, famines and earthquakes, and even the gospel proclaimed through the whole earth was fulfilled in the first century before A.D. 70 when the temple was destroyed.

Some theologians will even admit this fact of fulfillment. But in an attempt to hold onto their futurism, they claim that when Jesus spoke about the "abomination of desolation," he was jumping ahead in time thousands of years to the end of history when the Antichrist is supposed to appear.

Surprise, surprise, this is another case of mistaken identity. Let's uncover the real secret culprit.

Chapter 11
Abomination of Desolation

When futurists read about the abomination of desolation in Jesus' prophecy, they see it as the Antichrist, the Beast, or some other demonic person in our own future who has yet to appear and set foot in the temple in Jerusalem (which is supposedly yet to be rebuilt). This is supposed to happen in the midst of the great tribulation and heralds a betrayal of a treaty made between the Antichrist and Israel. It is at this point that the true nature of this character is supposed to be revealed. Let's take a look at the entire passage to get the context.

> Matthew 24:15–28
> So when you see the abomination of desolation spoken of by the prophet Daniel, standing in the holy place (let the reader understand), [16] then let those who are in Judea flee to the mountains. [17] Let the one who is on the housetop not go down to take what is in his house, [18] and let the one who is in the field not turn back to take his cloak. [19] And alas for women who are pregnant and for those who are nursing infants in those days! [20] Pray that your flight may not be in winter or on a Sabbath. [21] For then there will be great tribulation, such as has not been from the beginning of the world until now, no, and never will be. [22] And if those days had not been cut short, no human being would be saved. But for the sake of the elect those days will be cut short. [23] Then if anyone says to you, 'Look, here is the Christ!' or 'There he is!' do not believe it. [24] For false christs and false prophets will arise and perform great signs and wonders, so as to lead astray, if possible, even the elect. [25] See, I have told you beforehand. [26] So, if they say to you, 'Look, he is in the wilderness,' do not go out. If they say, 'Look, he is in the

> inner rooms,' do not believe it. [27] For as the lightning comes from the east and shines as far as the west, so will be the coming of the Son of Man. [28] Wherever the corpse is, there the vultures will gather.

As the reader can see, we have already discussed much in this passage. We have already seen the fulfillment of the false christs and false prophets in the wilderness as occurring during the build up to the Roman war with the Jews in A.D. 66. We saw that the great tribulation was considered by the apostle John to be in process by the time he wrote the book of Revelation, sometime before the temple was destroyed. So to wrench the abomination of desolation out of that context and suggest that it will occur thousands of years later is to do violence to the text and context of the prophecy.

But if the abomination of desolation took place in that time period and not in our future, then who or what was it? Jesus gave us a clue when he said that it was "spoken of by the prophet Daniel" (Matt 24:15). So let's go back to see if Daniel gave us any answers.

Spoken of by Daniel

Daniel wrote about the abomination of desolation in three places, Daniel 9:26-27; 11:31; 12:11. I will not have the space to explore this topic fully because it is quite complex. It is one of those prophecies that has a hundred different interpretations. I recommend *The Seventy Weeks and the Great Tribulation* by Philip Mauro online. Some Bible scholars suggest that the abomination of desolation spoken of in all three passages is the same being. Others argue that they are not the same and that the term "abomination of desolation" is another generic metaphor that means any unholy, earthly power that desecrates God's holy temple. I tend toward this interpretation. But rather than argue those fine details, I want to focus in on one passage in this discourse that almost everyone agrees on. It is the passage in Daniel's prophecy of the seventy weeks.

The Seventy Weeks

Probably the most famous messianic prophecy in the Old Testament is Daniel's prophecy of the seventy weeks. This is because it predicts the coming Messiah within a specific number of years from a specific historical event—the decree to restore and rebuild Jerusalem, most likely fulfilled in the decree of Artaxerxes I around 458 B.C. (Neh 2:1). The seventy weeks is actually "seventy sevens" of years, or 490 years, and it would place Messiah approximately in the very lifetime of Jesus.[1] This is why the messianic expectation was so high in the first century. Let's take a brief look at this prophecy.

> Daniel 9:24–27
> Seventy weeks are decreed about your people and your holy city, to finish the transgression, to put an end to sin, and to atone for iniquity, to bring in everlasting righteousness, to seal both vision and prophet, and to anoint a most holy place. [25] Know therefore and understand that from the going out of the word to restore and build Jerusalem to the coming of an anointed one, a prince, there shall be seven weeks. Then for sixty-two weeks it shall be built again with squares and moat, but in a troubled time. [26] And after the sixty-two weeks, an anointed one shall be cut off and shall have nothing. And the people of the prince who is to come shall destroy the city and the sanctuary. Its end shall come with a flood, and to the end there shall be war. Desolations are decreed. [27] And he shall make a strong covenant with many for one week, and for half of the week he shall put an end to sacrifice and offering. And on the wing of abominations shall come one who makes desolate, until the decreed end is poured out on the desolator.

Daniel's prophecy was given to Israel. Because Israel had been unfaithful to Yahweh, he had punished his people with exile in Babylon, where Daniel was writing from. When he wrote of "finishing the transgression, to put an end to sin and atone for iniquity," he was writing about the sin of Israel. When Messiah came, he would put an end to sin and atone for it. This was fulfilled when the angel of the Lord told Mary to call her child Jesus, "for he will save his people from their sins" (Matt 1:21).

---

[1] Another theory is that the decree to restore and rebuild Jerusalem was that of Cyrus the Great of Babylon in 538 B.C., which would still place Messiah in the rough time period of Jesus. The prophecy does not claim scientific precision, but rather approximate eras.

When Jesus cried out "It is finished" on the cross, he was putting an end to sin with his once-for-all sacrifice that atoned for iniquity and brought in everlasting righteousness, just as Daniel prophesied (Heb 9:12-14).

Jesus confirmed the promise, or "sealed both vision and prophet" (Dan 9:24) in fulfilling the messianic promise that all the prophets had looked forward to (1 Pet 1:10-12).

The city of Jerusalem was rebuilt as the prophecy said within the first seven sevens, or 49 years, during the "troubled times" of Nehemiah (Neh 4:18). Then, after the next sixty-two sevens of years, or about 483 years later, the prophecy predicted that an anointed one (*messiah*, in Hebrew), would be "cut off and shall have nothing" (Dan 9:26). We see this fulfilled in Jesus' words on the cross, "My God, my God, why have you forsaken me?" (Matt 27:46, taken from Psalm 22:1). "For our sake he made [Jesus] to be sin who knew no sin, so that in him we might become the righteousness of God" (2 Cor 5:21).

Then we are told that a people of a "prince to come" shall destroy the city and sanctuary (Jerusalem and the temple). This prince is linked with "desolations" and coming "on the wing of abominations" (Dan 9:26-27). This prince is the abomination of desolation. But the next verse presents an interpretive problem. We read that "he" shall make a covenant with many for one week, and for half of the week, he shall put an end to sacrifice and offering" (v. 27). Most futurists interpret this person to be the Antichrist, and that last week of years is the seven year tribulation. This Antichrist supposedly makes a treaty with Israel that he breaks after three-and-a-half years. And then he puts an end to sacrifices in a rebuilt temple in Jerusalem.

But the grammar of the text does not necessitate this interpretation. In fact, the "he" referred to in verse 27 can grammatically be a reference, not to the "prince of desolations," but to the anointed one (Messiah). As scholar Kenneth Gentry wrote,

> The indefinite pronoun "he" does not refer back to "the prince who is to come" of verse 26. That "prince" is a subordinate noun; the "people" is the dominant noun. Thus, the "he" refers back to the last dominant individual mentioned: "Messiah" (v. 26a). The Messiah is the leading figure in the whole prophecy, so that even the destruction of the Temple is

> related to His death. In fact, the people who destroy the Temple are providentially "His armies" (Matt. 22:2-7).[2]

Let's reread the Daniel prophecy with this clearer insight.

> Daniel 9:27
> And he [Messiah] shall make a strong covenant with many for one week, and for half of the week he shall put an end to sacrifice and offering. And on the wing of abominations shall come one who makes desolate, until the decreed end is poured out on the desolator."

The three-and-a-half years ("half of the week") is not in the middle of a future tribulation; it represents the approximately three-and-a-half years of Christ's ministry. In the Bible Satan does not make covenants; God does. The strong covenant is not of the Antichrist; it is the new covenant of the Christ. It is not the Antichrist who puts an end to sacrifice and offering. The earlier verse already said it was Messiah who would put an end to sin. It was Jesus Christ's sacrifice that put an end to sacrifices and offerings, once and for all (Heb 10:12), not some future Antichrist.

Then sometime after this messianic sacrifice, the abomination of desolation would come and destroy the city and sanctuary like a flood. Though there are many issues to address in this passage, the main thrust of it focuses around the Messiah and the destruction of Jerusalem and the temple, which we know occurred by A.D. 70. We know that historically the people of the Roman general Titus ("the prince who is to come") did in fact destroy the city and sanctuary. And it took place around the time period of Messiah.

Most futurists, because of their preconceived eschatology, separate the abomination of desolation from the coming of Messiah. They think that the prophecy is talking about the first coming of Jesus and then jumps ahead thousands of years into the future to talk about an Antichrist who is the abomination of desolation. They have to stick a two thousand year gap into the Daniel prophecy, which simply isn't there. The context consistently fits the first century where all those things occurred.

---

[2] Dr. Kenneth L. Gentry, Jr., "Daniel's Seventy Weeks," (Covenant Media Foundation). http://www.cmfnow.com/articles/pt551.htm

And if you don't believe me, let's ask Jesus.

Back to Jesus

The book of Matthew was written to Jews. Because of this it has many Hebraisms and Old Testament references and concepts that most Jews would know when reading them. But the book of Luke was written more for a Gentile audience, so he tended to explain things or translate them for the non-Hebrew audience. The abomination of desolation is one of those things he translated for us.

Luke 21 and Mark 13 both contain the same sermon also found in Matthew 24. But there are some variations in the text. Let me put them side by side so you can see the obvious correlation.

Matthew 24:15–16	Luke 21:20–22	Mark 13:14
[15] "So when you see the abomination of desolation spoken of by the prophet Daniel, standing in the holy place (let the reader understand), [16] then let those who are in Judea flee to the mountains.	[20] "But when you see Jerusalem surrounded by armies, then know that its desolation has come near. [21] Then let those who are in Judea flee to the mountains.	[14] "But when you see the abomination of desolation standing where he ought not to be (let the reader understand), then let those who are in Judea flee to the mountains.

The Hebrew image of "abomination of desolation" in Matthew and Mark is translated by Luke to be "when you see Jerusalem surrounded by armies." So, Jesus himself told us that the correct interpretation of "abomination of desolation" is Jerusalem being surrounded by armies. In A.D. 69 the abominable Roman armies did in fact surround Jerusalem, just like Jesus said. In this sense, they were "standing in a holy place" around the holy city, "where he [Titus, the abominable "prince" of those armies] ought not to be." Titus, with his Roman legions, was the abomination of desolation. When I first read this explanation by Luke, I was blown away. It could not be more clear. Talk about Jesus himself giving us a key to the interpretation of a prophecy.

Once again, the destruction of the city and temple were a main focus of the prophetic near future for Jesus and the apostles. In fact, at another time, Jesus referred to the destruction of the city of Jerusalem as punishment for the Jews not recognizing the time of the visitation of God in Messiah.

Luke 19:41–44
And when he drew near [Jerusalem] and saw the city, he wept over it, [42] saying, "Would that you, even you, had known on this day the things that make for peace! But now they are hidden from your eyes. [43] For the days will come upon you, when your enemies will set up a barricade around you and surround you and hem you in on every side [44] and tear you down to the ground, you and your children within you. And they will not leave one stone upon another in you, because you did not know the time of your visitation."

Remember the language that Jesus used in Matthew 24 about God not leaving one stone of the temple upon another? Well, he used it here again, linking those two prophecies about the destruction that was coming in A.D. 70. At that time the Romans set up a barricade all around Jerusalem, just like Jesus said they would. They surrounded the city on every side (just like Jesus predicted), and they tore down both city and temple to the ground, not leaving one stone of that temple upon another (just like Jesus prophesied). The abomination that brought desolation to Jerusalem and the temple is not a prophecy of our future but a fulfillment of our past.

More Great Tribulation

What Jesus said after the abomination of desolation is revelatory. He told his disciples that if they were in Judea when the abomination (Rome) came, they should flee to the mountains (24:16). He gave them instructions on how to avoid being caught up in the judgment upon Jerusalem.

Matthew 24:17–22
Let the one who is on the housetop not go down to take what is in his house, [18] and let the one who is in the field not turn back to take his cloak. [19] And alas for women who are pregnant and for those who are nursing infants in those days! [20] Pray that your flight may not be in winter or on a Sabbath. [21] For then there will be great tribulation, such as has not been from the beginning of the world until now, no, and never will be. [22] And if those days had not been cut

short, no human being would be saved. But for the sake of the elect those days will be cut short.

We looked at the "unequalled" great tribulation earlier and discovered that it was a reference used of the past destruction of Jerusalem and the temple by Babylon. Now that same kind of thing would happen again. Luke added these words to Jesus' prophetic Olivet Discourse.

Luke 21:23–24
Alas for women who are pregnant and for those who are nursing infants in those days! For there will be great distress upon the earth and wrath against this people. 24 They will fall by the edge of the sword and be led captive among all nations, and Jerusalem will be trampled underfoot by the Gentiles."

In A.D. 70, Jerusalem was trampled underfoot by the Gentiles, just as Jesus said it would be. The Jews experienced great wrath, fell by the edge of the sword, and were led captive among the nations, just as Jesus said. Josephus' *War of the Jews* recorded the miseries and suffering in stark fulfillment of these prophecies.

Josephus, *Wars of the Jews* (2.465)
It was then common to see cities filled with dead bodies, still lying unburied, and those of old men, mixed with infants, all dead, and scattered about together; women also lay amongst them, without any covering for their nakedness: you might then see the whole province full of inexpressible calamities, while the dread of still more barbarous practices which were threatened, was everywhere greater than what had been already perpetrated.[3]

(6.275-276)
Yet was the misery itself more terrible than this disorder; for one would have thought that the hill itself, on which the temple stood, was seething hot, as full of fire on every part

---

[3] Flavius Josephus and William Whiston, *The Works of Josephus: Complete and Unabridged* (Peabody: Hendrickson, 1987).

> of it, that the blood was larger in quantity than the fire, and those that were slain more in number than those that slew them; for the ground did nowhere appear visible, for the dead bodies that lay on it; but the soldiers went over heaps of these bodies, as they ran upon such as fled from them.[4]
>
> (6.428-429)
> Now this vast multitude is indeed collected out of remote places, but the entire nation was now shut up by fate as in a prison, and the Roman army encompassed the city when it was crowded with inhabitants. Accordingly the multitude of those that therein perished exceeded all the destructions that either men or God ever brought upon the world; for, to speak only of what was publicly known, the Romans slew some of them, some they carried captives.[5]
>
> (6.420-421)
> Now the number of those that were carried captive during this whole war was collected to be ninety-seven thousand; as was the number of those that perished during the whole siege eleven hundred thousand, the greater part of whom were indeed of the same nation [with the citizens of Jerusalem], but not belonging to the city itself.[6]

It is interesting that Josephus, a Jew, though not a Christian, used the same hyperbolic terminology of the siege of Jerusalem that Jesus used of the great tribulation and siege of Jerusalem. Josephus wrote that the number of those who perished "exceeded all the destructions that either men or God ever brought upon the world." This reinforces my earlier argument that this "nothing like it" language is not literal, but rather deliberately poetic to instill a sense of the spiritual importance of the event.

---

[4] Flavius Josephus and William Whiston, *The Works of Josephus.*
[5] Flavius Josephus and William Whiston, *The Works of Josephus.*
[6] Flavius Josephus and William Whiston, *The Works of Josephus.*

Flee to the Mountains

In this context of Roman barbarism and unholy abomination, Jesus gave the directive to his followers to "flee to the mountains." Why? Because the destruction of Jerusalem that was coming was God's judgment on the Jews for rejecting Jesus. But the Christians did not reject him, so Jesus wanted his chosen people to escape before that judgment fell.

And escape they did. Early church historian Eusebius recorded how the Christians followed Jesus' warnings.

> Eusebius, Ecclesiastical History 3:5
> But the people of the church in Jerusalem had been commanded by a revelation, vouchsafed to approved men there before the war, to leave the city and to dwell in a certain town of Perea called Pella. And when those that believed in Christ had come thither from Jerusalem, then, as if the royal city of the Jews and the whole land of Judea were entirely destitute of holy men, the judgment of God at length overtook those who had committed such outrages against Christ and his apostles, and totally destroyed that generation of impious men.[7]

My second book in the *Chronicles of the Apocalypse* series, Remnant: Rescue of the Elect tells this story in dramatic fiction. The Christians were spared from God's judgment because they were no longer part of the old system, the old age of the old covenant. God was destroying the temple as the incarnation of that old covenant. Since the Jews did not embrace the new covenant, they were in a dead religion. The Roman army was like vultures gathering around the carcass of that dead religion to finish it off, just like Jesus said in Matthew 24:28.

> Matthew 24:28
> Wherever the corpse is, there the vultures will gather.

---

[7] Eusebius of Caesaria, "The Church History of Eusebius," in *Eusebius: Church History, Life of Constantine the Great, and Oration in Praise of Constantine*, ed. Philip Schaff and Henry Wace, trans. Arthur Cushman McGiffert, vol. 1, *A Select Library of the Nicene and Post-Nicene Fathers of the Christian Church, Second Series* (New York: Christian Literature Company, 1890), 138.

Chapter 12
The Antichrist and the Beast

Throughout this book we have been working through Matthew 24, verse by verse. Since we just looked at the abomination of desolation, I want to take a chapter to discuss a couple of issues related to this abomination that are not actually in Mathew 24: the Antichrist and the Beast. I am doing this for two reasons. First, they are very popular issues in Bible prophecy circles that many link to the abomination of desolation we just examined. Second, these are also key elements that show up in my novel series, *Chronicles of the Apocalypse* (Book One: *Tyrant – Rise of the Beast*). This book you are reading is a theological explanation of the narrative for the *Chronicles of the Apocalypse*, so I owe it to the readers of the series.

Antichrist

As I have indicated several times throughout this book, I had for the longest time unquestionably accepted the teaching about a future, individual Antichrist, a politically influential leader who would rise up in a time of geopolitical turmoil to "save" the world. He would make a covenant with Israel, only to break it and unleash hell on earth. It seemed to make sense that this character would be equated with the abomination of desolation, and some teachers even linked him to the Beast, another well-known speculation of end times researchers.

In fact, whole books have been written about all kinds of details that prophecy pundits seem certain this Antichrist will do. When I was challenged to look at the Bible verses that actually talk about antichrist, I discovered that antichrist is *not* an individual; and the Bible never talks about it as being in the future, but in the first century!

There are exactly four verses in the Bible that mention antichrist. You read that right. Only four verses. Judging by the amount of books written on this word alone, you'd think it was a major doctrine in the Bible. Let's take a look at each one of the four verses to see what I began to learn.

> 1 John 2:18
> Children, it is the last hour, and as you have heard that antichrist is coming, so now many antichrists have come. Therefore we know that it is the last hour.
>
> 1 John 2:22
> Who is the liar but he who denies that Jesus is the Christ? This is the antichrist, he who denies the Father and the Son.
>
> 1 John 4:3
> and every spirit that does not confess Jesus is not from God. This is the spirit of the antichrist, which you heard was coming and now is in the world already.
>
> 2 John 7
> For many deceivers have gone out into the world, those who do not confess the coming of Jesus Christ in the flesh. Such a one is the deceiver and the antichrist.

So the first thing I noticed was that only the apostle John used the term "antichrist," not any other Old Testament or New Testament author. Despite the claim by some that the Antichrist is the abomination of desolation of Daniel 9 and Matthew 24 or that he is the "man of lawlessness" in 2 Thessalonians 2:3, these are all creative speculations without direct proof of connection. Ultimately they are linked not by the text but by the preconceived end times scheme.

What about the fact that John also wrote Revelation, the quintessential eschatological sermon? The first thing you might think is that the Antichrist is the Beast. Well, actually, there are two beasts, a sea beast and a land beast; but we'll get to that later. Right now, the problem is that John, that apostle who wrote these epistles *and* the book of Revelation, chose never to use the term "antichrist" for any of the characters in Revelation—not for the land beast or for the sea beast or for any of those demonic beasts that fight against God in the apocalypse. That single fact was enough to make me stop and read the verses a little closer to see why a term that John would use four times in two letters would never show up in his magnum opus on the end times.

When it comes to Bible interpretation, some things are just not clear. Understanding these things requires internal biblical study and outside information. One of the rules of interpretation is that when a text defines a word, you can have strong clarity of what the author meant by that word. In this case, the apostle told us exactly what he meant by "antichrist," and it is specifically and explicitly *not* an individual incarnation of Satan or Satan's child or any *one* person that futurists say he is.

Antichrist is not an individual, historical or political character at all. It is a term that describes *anyone* who is against Christ. John defined the term three times in those four verses! In the Bible when God wanted to make a point, he repeated himself. In this case, it's almost as if God was anticipating the speculations of modern prophecy prognosticators and deliberately told us ahead of time that they are all wrong. John wrote explicitly that *anyone* who denies Jesus or does not confess him as coming in the flesh is an enemy of Christ, or antichrist. That's what the term meant to him—"anti" (against) Christ, a special demonic attitude of hatred that results in violence. Christians were being persecuted by Jews who denied that the Messiah (Christ) came in the flesh. Those Jews were against Christ—antichrist. Christians were being persecuted by the Roman empire for not obeying Caesar. Rome was antichrist. But worst of all, John was warning against those false teachers who had gone out from the church and turned against it. Those false teachers were deceiving the body of Christ about Jesus, sin, salvation, and works (1 John 3:7-10). Those false teachers were antichrist. That is why John said there were *many* antichrists who *had already come* (2:18). Those antichrists "went out from us, but they were not of us" (2:19). That spirit of antichrist was "in the world already" (4:3) in those who denied Christ explicitly or doctrinally. Antichrist cannot be an historical figure yet in our future because John says that antichrist was *already there in his day*. And he even said that the presence of this demonic hostility against Christ was proof that it was the "last hour" (2:18) of those last days we looked at earlier.

This is no different than how we use the term "anti" today. We may say someone is an anti-Semite because he is against Jews or that someone is anti-Christian when he is against Christians. There is no single individual called "the anti-Semite." Anyone who hates Jews is an anti-Semite. So, the anti-Semite is the one who hates Jews or denies their history.

But "antichrist" is not only a term used of humans but also used of spirits. And *any* spirit that does not confess Jesus is considered antichrist (1 John 4:3). This is not a single, individual spirit, but many spirits that have that title.

When faced with this obvious, explicit definition, some futurists say that there is still a single, individual, historical, political figure called *the* Antichrist who is yet to come and that people who deny Christ are forerunners of that individual by having the same satanic spirit. But this is not what the text actually says. The text does not say that there is an individual called *the* Antichrist and many little antichrists who foreshadow him. It simply says anyone and everyone who denies Jesus is *the* antichrist, not just one individual (1 John 2:22; 4:3; 2 John 7). "The antichrist" is a term used by John for each and every one of the many antichrists.

According to the apostle John, the antichrist was the spirit or mentality of those who denied Christ. Antichrist had already come in his day and was proof to him that the last days had arrived in his lifetime (2:18).

So, there was an abomination of desolation and even an individual "man of lawlessness" in John's day, but they were not *the* Antichrist because there is no individual, historical, political Antichrist in Scripture, only many antichrists who denied Jesus.

What about that other fascination of end times pundits, the Beast of Revelation?

The Beast

Who is the Beast of Revelation? This is a question that has perplexed prophecy pundits for two millennia. In my own lifetime, I've seen so many options offered that it is laughable—from Henry Kissinger to Ronald Reagan, to Barrack Obama, and on and on. Every few years it's someone new. And thanks to that classic movie *The Omen*, we're all looking to see if he has three sixes as a birthmark.

The only problem is there isn't one Beast but two, a sea beast (Rev 13:1) and a land beast (Rev 13:11). So, once again, we see another assumed concept about the end times that is not biblically accurate and results in all kinds of misunderstandings that reign like little monsters in modern prophecy circles. What most people are usually referring to when they say, "the Beast" is the sea beast.

Since this topic requires an examination of the book of Revelation, and I don't have the space to deal with it thoroughly, I will first recommend a full-length treatment by Kenneth Gentry entitled *The Beast of Revelation*. (You can get it free online here.) Gentry is an eminent biblical scholar whose new Revelation commentary, *The Divorce of Israel*, is a game changer in Revelation interpretation.

There are many different aspects of the Beast and the book of Revelation that need to be addressed. But for this chapter, I want to focus on the few scriptural arguments that are the strongest ones that persuaded me that the Beast of Revelation is not some future ally of a future Antichrist. Rather, he is both an historical king and kingdom that occurred in the first century when John predicted he would.

The Beast of Revelation was Nero Caesar.

I thought I'd get that out of the way so you wouldn't be kept in suspense. Now, if you are like I was when I first heard such a thing, you may be thinking to yourself, "Outrageous! That can't be!" And you may even be scrambling to some Bible passages to prove to yourself that Nero could not have fulfilled all those passages. Chances are, you haven't been taught the truth about this.

The problem here is that futurist speculations about the Beast are precisely that, speculations. Since they all assume that Revelation was written about a far-distant future scenario instead of a near first century one, they cannot accept the possibility that it was already fulfilled in John's day.

But what if the book of Revelation made actual time references to the fulfillment of the Beast in John's own lifetime? What if there were internal scriptural references to the first century that said the Beast was in John's own day?

Believe it or not, there are. Let me show you a few of them.

The Time is Near

In the very first verses of Revelation, John explained that the things in the book "must soon take place."

> Revelation 1:1–3
> The revelation of Jesus Christ, which God gave him to show to his servants the things that must soon take place. He made it known by sending his angel to his servant John, [2] who bore witness to the word of God and to the testimony of Jesus Christ, even to all that he saw. [3] Blessed is the one who reads aloud the words of this prophecy, and blessed are those who hear, and who keep what is written in it, for the time is near.

Try as they may, futurists cannot turn the meaning of the words "soon" and "near" into "thousands of years from now." The notion that "a day is as a thousand years to the Lord," just doesn't cut it. John was not writing to an unknown generation of Christians in the future. He was writing to seven churches in Asia Minor who were undergoing the great tribulation in their day (Rev 1:9), persecuted and martyred for their faith. It would be a lie if he was telling them to persevere because these things were about to take place soon, but he really meant it for someone else *thousands of years from now*. After all, the letter was written to encourage the readers of his generation.

Remember when Jesus talked about "this generation" of his listeners seeing "all these things," including the abomination of desolation? And remember how he bookended the discourse with the same phrase, "This generation will not pass away until all these things take place?" Jesus used repetition to stress the all-inclusive fulfillment within his own generation. Well, John did the same thing. We saw that he wrote in the beginning of his letter that the things he was about to tell them, including the Beast, would soon take place because the time was near. Then at the end of the letter, he repeated himself when Jesus told him,

> Revelation 22:10
> Do not seal up the words of the prophecy of this book, for the time is near.

God was repeating himself to make the point. He wanted those churches of the first century to have patience with their suffering because God was about to pour out his judgment on those who persecuted them and vindicate Jesus' claim to Messiah. Saying that the time was near at the beginning and end of the letter stressed the fact that those things were to begin happening within the lifetime of his readers, not thousands of years in the future.

In an interesting comparison of Scripture, the angel that gave Daniel's vision of end times prophecy told him something different.

> Daniel 12:4
> But you, Daniel, shut up the words and seal the book, until the time of the end.

So we see that when a prophecy was not to occur for thousands of years, the angel said to "seal up the book" (Dan 12:4); but when a prophecy was about to occur near the lifetime of the prophet, he said, "Do not seal up the book" (Rev 22:10). If John's Revelation was to occur thousands of years later in our modern time period, the angel would have said to seal up the book; but he did not. He said to keep it open because the time was near for those things to begin happening. "Near" does not mean "far."

The Beast was about to be revealed in John's own day.

The Sixth King

The second historical reference that roots the Beast of Revelation irrefutably in the first century is John's time reference about the sixth king in Revelation 17:10. Let me set the context for the passage. John wrote that he was about to explain the sea beast of Revelation 13:1 that had seven heads and on whom the harlot rode. He said that "the beast that you saw was, and is not, and is to come" (17:8) in a perverse parody of God (who was and is and is to come, Rev 4:8).

What exactly does this phrase mean, "was and is not and is to come"? John told us.

> Revelation 17:9–10
> This calls for a mind with wisdom: the seven heads are seven mountains on which the woman is seated; [10] they are also seven kings, five of whom have fallen, one is, the other has not yet come, and when he does come he must remain only a little while.

Here we have a passage where John explicitly related his vision to what was occurring in his own day. He indicated that the Beast is both a kingdom and a king. It is a kingdom in that its seven heads are seven mountains. Rome was well known in John's day as the city on seven hills or mountains. So he was talking about the Roman empire. Then he spoke of the kings of that empire; and "king" was another word for "Caesar" (John 19:15).

John said that of seven kings of that kingdom, five have fallen (died), the sixth one is (currently alive and reigning), and the seventh is yet to come (after the current one dies—"is not"). Modern prophecy pundits read this as some kind of arcane reference to a succession of future kings. But to the readers of John's day, it would have been obvious whom he was talking about. Nero was the sixth king of Rome at the time of his writing ("now is"). As ancient Roman historians like Suetonius have written, Nero was the sixth king of Rome. The previous five were Julius, Augustus, Tiberius, Gaius, and Claudius. And in yet another clear fulfillment of John's words in his own day, the Caesar after Nero was Galba, who reigned a mere seven months. In other words, "only a little while," just as John said he would (17:10).[1]

John's historical time reference to the Caesars of his own day sets the Beast in the first century. That little reference to "now is" clearly communicates that it was happening in John's day.

666: the Number of His Name

Thanks to futurist prophecy prognosticators, many aspects of the Beast have been so severely distorted from the original scriptural context that people assume unbiblical things about it. The number of the Beast is one of those misunderstood assumptions.

The text in question is this:

---

[1] "We find this order of emperors also in Josephus (Ant. 19:1:11 §75; cp. 18:2:2 §32–33; 18:6:10 §224); …On this reckoning, the five that have "fallen" would be Julius through Claudius. That they are "fallen [epesen]" alludes "to the eminent rank of those whose death is declared" as in 2Sa 3:38. TDNT (6:161) notes that this word is commonly used of dying, particularly in the LXX (cf. Prignet 493). The sixth one who "is" (Gk.: estin, 17:10b) would be Nero. Regarding the seventh who will come and "must remain a little while [oligon auton dei meinai]" we should note that following Nero's thirteen year rule Galba takes the reins of government. But he rules for only seven months (June, AD 68 —January, AD 69), the shortest reigning emperor to that time." Ken Gentry, "Revelation 17:9-10" *The Divorce of Israel: A Redemptive-Historical Interpretation of Revelation*, unpublished draft (Liberty Alliance, 2015).

> Revelation 13:18
> This calls for wisdom: let the one who has understanding calculate the number of the beast, for it is the number of a man, and his number is 666.

There is no 666 birthmark on the Antichrist. And the number is not three sixes in a row as many Christians mistakenly believe. It is a *numerical value* of six hundred and sixty six. So it cannot be three sixes in a row on something like a barcode. And it could never have been Ronald Wilson Reagan just because he has six letters in each name. Rather, it's a symbolic number with historical reference.

What John was doing here is called *gematria*, and it was a known practice in the ancient world. Gematria was the cryptic computation of numerical values of words. Ancient Greek and Hebrew did not have numbers as we do today with our Arabic numbering system. Their numbers were represented by letters of their alphabets. Each letter stood for a different numerical value. So when they wanted to be cryptic, clever, or creative, they would use gematria, as Gentry pointed out.

> In the midst of his Latin history, Suetonius records a sample of a Greek lampoon that was circulated after the burning of Rome, which occurred in A.D. 64… "A calculation new. Nero his mother slew." G J. C. Rolfe notes in the Loeb Classical Library edition of Suetonius's works that "the numerical value of the Greek letters in Nero's name (1005) is the same as that of the rest of the sentence; hence we have an equation, Nero = the slayer of his own mother." It is quite interesting to note that there were already anti-Nero cryptograms circulating when John wrote Revelation.[2]

"Wait a minute!" the insightful reader might say. "If the number of the Beast is 666 and if Gentry said that the number of Nero's name according to ancient Greek is 1005, then how could Nero be the Beast?"

---

[2] Ken Gentry, *The Beast of Revelation* (Tyler, TX: Instituted for Christian Economics, 1989, 1994), 32.

Good question. And the answer is because John was writing in Greek but he was thinking in Hebrew to further distance himself and his readers from their Roman oppressors. Nero's name in Hebrew actually does come out to 666, as Gentry explained.

> An ancient Hebrew spelling of Nero Caesar's name is קסר ןורנ (Nrwn Qsr). Archaeological finds from Murabba'at document this spelling in an Aramaic manuscript dating to the second year of Nero's reign. This spelling provides us with precisely the numerical value of 666, which is as follows: Nrwn: N =50; R =200; W =6; N =50 Qsr: Q =100; S =60; R =200.[3]

I suppose readers could convince themselves that this is all just a coincidence and surely there will be a future leader whose name will add up to six hundred and sixty six. But that would be like looking at a filled out crossword puzzle and saying, "No, there must be another way of answering those questions differently and still making the puzzle work."

It is not a coincidence that John used gematria in his day, during the time of Nero, and just happened by chance to put out a puzzle whose answer is Nero, the very king who was persecuting God's people with tribulation at that very moment. It is the most reasonable answer, indeed the only answer that really fits the original context of the author.

Someone may say, "Aha! If Nero was the Beast, when did he place a computer chip in the hands or heads of his followers? That surely never happened." This reveals another blind assumption of modern prophecy pundits. (Okay, I'm being a little facetious, but you get my point.)

Mark of the Beast

I want to cover this one last aspect of the Beast because it has absorbed the imagination of Christians for decades. Notions of a computer chip in the heads or hands of human worshipers of the Beast have raged in the

---

[3] Ken Gentry, "Revelation 13:18" *The Divorce of Israel: A Redemptive-Historical Interpretation of Revelation*, unpublished draft (Liberty Alliance, 2015).

predictions of so many teachers that it has become another assumption without biblical basis. Let me explain.

Understand that what I have to say here has no ties to any particular end times view. You can be a futurist of any stripe and still believe that the Scripture teaches what I am about to argue. We must let Scripture interpret Scripture, first and foremost.

Here is the actual text in Revelation.

> Revelation 13:16–17
> [The beast] causes all, both small and great, both rich and poor, both free and slave, to be marked on the right hand or the forehead, [17] so that no one can buy or sell unless he has the mark, that is, the name of the beast or the number of its name.

This notion of a mark is often taken literally, as if it is a UPC barcode tattoo (in the 1970s) or a GPS implant (in the 2000s). Futurists say that this fits perfectly with the technology we now have. But the problem is that the language of a mark already fit perfectly in the ancient world. What literalists miss is that the very next paragraph talks about the 144,000 followers of the Lamb who had the name of Jesus "and his Father's name written on their foreheads" (Rev 14:1). This "writing" is referred to as a symbolic "sealing" of the servants of God on their foreheads in Revelation 7:3.

The Bible student may remember that the notion of sealing is a spiritual metaphor of ownership, as in those sealed by the Holy Spirit (Eph 1:13). Revelation is comparing and contrasting those owned by the Beast with those owned by God.

But the reference to the hand and forehead is also a known metaphor rooted in the Old Testament, which the apostle John was drawing from in his own writings. When God told Moses to follow his commands, he said,

> Deuteronomy 6:6–8
> And these words that I command you today <u>shall be on your heart</u>. [7] You shall teach them diligently to your children, and shall talk of them when you sit in your house, and when you walk by the way, and when you lie down, and when you rise. [8] <u>You shall bind them as a sign on your hand, and they shall be as frontlets between your eyes</u>.

In this passage, God used the hand as a symbol of our behavior—what we do with our hands—and the forehead as a symbol of our mindset or thoughts. God wanted his people to treasure his Word in their hearts (another metaphor), to guide their every thought (forehead) and every action (hand).

The mark of the Beast is not a literal tattoo or computer chip, but a symbolic reference to ownership of those whose thoughts and behaviors are dictated by the Beast.

But what about the idea that they couldn't buy or sell without the mark? How does that come into play with this spiritualized ownership? Doesn't that refer to computer scanners used in a cashless society? Hardly.

In the days of John, there was something called the Imperial Cult of Caesar. In every Roman province, if not city, there was a requirement that all Roman subjects offer sacrifice to Caesar as a symbol of their submission to his authority.[4] The Jews were allowed to offer a sacrifice *on behalf of* Caesar in their temple in Jerusalem, rather than *to* Caesar.[5] It was a compromise that accommodated the fact that Jews could not perform such worship activities. This allowed them into the imperial cult under the loophole of a technicality. But they served the imperial cult nonetheless. Christians who did not participate in the imperial cult were economically and socially deprived. They could not engage in the trade guilds. They could not "buy and sell" because they did not perform the devotion to Caesar that marked them under his ownership.[6]

As N.T. Wright explained,

> The evidence now available, including that from epigraphy and archaeology, appears to show that the cult of Caesar, so far from being one new religion among many in the Roman

---

[4] S.F.R. Price, *Rituals and Power: The Roman Imperial Cult in Asia Minor* (Cambridge University Press, 1985), 248.

[5] Flavius Josephus, *The Wars of the Jews*, 2.409-410 (2.17.2).

[6] The Imperial Cult punishments on Christians is seen in the seven churches of Revelation, but it continued on into the next century as Tertullian writes about it as well: "You do not worship the gods," you say; "and you do not offer sacrifices for the emperors." Well, we do not offer sacrifice for others, for the same reason that we do not for ourselves,—namely, that your gods are not at all the objects of our worship. So we are accused of sacrilege and treason. This is the chief ground of charge against us." Tertullian, *"The Apology," in Latin Christianity: Its Founder, Tertullian*, ed. Alexander Roberts, James Donaldson, and A. Cleveland Coxe, trans. S. Thelwall, *vol. 3, The Ante-Nicene Fathers* (Buffalo, NY: Christian Literature Company, 1885), 26.

> world, had already by the time of Paul's missionary activity become not only the dominant cult in a large part of the empire, certainly in the parts where Paul was active, but was actually the means (as opposed to overt large-scale military presence) whereby the Romans managed to control and govern such huge areas as came under their sway. The emperor's far-off presence was made ubiquitous by the standard means of statues and coins (the latter being the principal mass medium of the ancient world), reflecting his image throughout his domains; he was the great benefactor, through whom the great blessings of justice and peace, and a host of lesser ones besides, were showered outwards upon the grateful populace — who in turn worshipped him, honored him, and paid him taxes.[7]

This brief introduction to the Beast of Revelation will no doubt raise more questions than it answers, but it opens the door to understanding that Beast in its first century context. For a detailed theological proof that Nero was the Beast of Revelation, check out Kenneth Gentry's free book, *The Beast of Revelation*, on my resources page. For a full rendering of how that monstrosity is played out in real history, see my novel Tyrant: Rise of the Beast, the first book in the *Chronicles of the Apocalypse* series.

For now, we must get back to the Matthew 24 passage and address the most controversial element of all, the climax of the entire prophecy.

[7] N.T. Wright, "Paul's Gospel and Caesar's Empire," in Ed. Richard A. Horsley, *Paul and Politics: Ekklesia, Israel, Imperium* (Penn., Trinity Press, 2000), 161.

Chapter 13
The Coming of the Son of Man

The second coming of Christ has probably been the most exciting prophecy to contemplate in my Christian life. Just picturing him coming on the clouds of heaven on his white horse, joined by his army of holy ones, has always caused me to rejoice at the glory of that day! And the very presence of this prophecy in the Olivet Discourse is what made me believe that it could only be in our future and not in the past. I mean, how clear can you get with the "plain language" of the Bible?

In fact, as I began to discover that all the other prophecies of Matthew 24 were actually fulfilled in the first century—false prophets, persecution, temple judgment, great tribulation, and abomination of desolation—it created a cognitive dissonance in me. Christ obviously did not come back in the first century, so why would there be a big gap in the prediction between the end of the old covenant age and the return of Christ thousands of years later? I did what some scholars and theologians have done; I held onto my preconceived bias. I resolved the rational tension by concluding that somehow the first part of Matthew 24 was about the first century destruction of the temple and the last part jumped from then to the end of history when Jesus returned. I created a split prophecy. And maybe that would allow me to say that it was somewhat fulfilled in the first century, but will all be fulfilled again in a double fulfillment later in our future.

But the text would soon reveal to me that was not possible. And I would begin to understand the biblical meaning of Christ coming in glory and how different it was from my hyperliteralized modernism. The funny thing was, this was no secret, esoteric revelation. It was all there in the text, plain as day, and always had been. I had just been blinded by my Western, futurist bias.

Timing Is Everything

Try as I may, I could not find a separation in the prior prophecies regarding the coming of the Son of Man that concluded the discourse. Right after Jesus described the abomination of desolation and the destruction of the city and temple, he warned his disciples again about false christs. And then he compared those "comings" of christs with the coming of the Son of Man.

> Matthew 24:27
> For as the lightning comes from the east and shines as far as the west, so will be the coming of the Son of Man.

In other words, he told his disciples what his true coming would be like, so they would not be deceived by others. Remember, he had also said that the generation he was speaking to was not going to pass away before all these things took place.

But then he said even more.

> Matthew 24:29–30
> Immediately after the tribulation of those days the sun will be darkened, and the moon will not give its light, and the stars will fall from heaven, and the powers of the heavens will be shaken. [30] Then will appear in heaven the sign of the Son of Man, and then all the tribes of the earth will mourn, and they will see the Son of Man coming on the clouds of heaven with power and great glory.

Immediately after the tribulation of those days. So all that tribulation—that he had previously described would happen to them—would be *immediately* followed by the cosmic catastrophes and then his "coming on the clouds." Not thousands of years later, but immediately after that tribulation. This passage could not be cut in half, with the first half taking place in his generation and the other half taking place many generations later. It was one continuous flowing series of consecutive events to occur before his generation passed away.

Of course, that was still difficult to accept because it just could not be that Jesus came in the first century! And all those cosmic catastrophes obviously did not happen.

Or did they?

Cosmic Catastrophes

In chapter 5, we already studied what the Old Testament meant when it described the sun and moon being darkened and the stars falling from the sky. That was poetic imagery describing the fall of earthly powers and the spiritual powers behind them. When a kingdom was overthrown it was described in decreation terms of the created order going dark. So it would make perfect sense that Jesus—saturated as he was in Old Testament narrative and imagery—would use the same exact language to describe the overthrow of Jerusalem, the temple, and the Jewish leaders that the Old Testament prophets used to describe the first overthrow of Jerusalem the temple and the Jewish leaders. That abomination of desolation, the Roman emperor and his armies, would surround the city walls and destroy Jerusalem, not leaving one stone of the temple upon another. That event is marked as a fall of a nation and its leaders: the darkening of the sun and moon with falling stars.

But what of the shaking of the heavens? Was that a literal earthquake or another metaphor?

The Shaking of the Heavens

Actually, the text says that "the powers of the heavens will be shaken," which reinforces the notion of a spiritual analogy of heavenly powers, not an earthly quake. In chapter 5 we saw that the destruction of the first temple in 539 B.C. by Babylon was described as including the heavens trembling (Joel 2:10) and God punishing the host of heaven (Isa 24:21). When Edom was destroyed it was described as "the skies roll up like a scroll," and "the host of heaven shall rot away" (Isa 34:2-4). So a shaking of the heavens was no new idea to Jesus, and it was commonly understood as figurative language for the fall of great powers, governments, and authorities.

But the New Testament adds a fascinating explanation of this "shaking of the heavens and the earth" as a poetic metaphor for the new covenant. The writer of the book of Hebrews depicted the removal of the old covenant with its replacement by the new covenant as a shaking of the heavens and earth.

In Hebrews 12:24, the author explained that believers have come to Jesus, the mediator of a new covenant, something superior to the old covenant. It turns out that covenants are a kind of shaking.

> Hebrews 12:26–28
> At that time [Mosaic old covenant] his voice shook the earth, but now he has promised, "Yet once more I will shake not only the earth but also the heavens." [27] This phrase, "Yet once more," indicates the removal of things that are shaken—that is, things that have been made—in order that the things that cannot be shaken may remain. [28] Therefore let us be grateful for receiving a kingdom that cannot be shaken, and thus let us offer to God acceptable worship, with reverence and awe.

Here the author described the change of covenants from old to new as a shaking of the earth and the heavens. The destruction of the temple was a physical expression of the spiritual reality of the covenantal heavens being shaken, the guiding theme of the entire passage of Matthew 24. Shaking the heavens meant a transformation of the covenantal order. The New Testament "heavens" cannot be shaken because it is the final, permanent covenant through Jesus the promised Messiah.

Revelation scholar Ken Gentry summarizes the progression of this covenantal kingdom transformation:

> The New Testament records the gradual establishing (Mt 13:31–33; Mk 4:26–29) of the kingdom. It traces its development from its ministerial announcement (Mk 1:15; Mt 12:28) to its legal securing at the cross (Mt 28:18; Ro 1:3–4; Php 2:1–11; Col 1:13; 2:14–15) to its public vindication and final establishment in Israel's overthrow (Mt 23:32–24:21; Gal 4:21–31; 1Th 2:16; Rev 5–1). God's removal of the temple system—physically breaking down the "dividing wall of hostility" legally broken in Christ (Eph 2:14)—conclusively ended the early Zionistic tendencies of many first-century Christians (e.g., Ac 11:1–3; 15:1; Ro

> 14:1–8; Gal 1–5; Col 2:16; Tit 3:9) and established Christianity as a separate religion in its own right.[1]

So now everything in the Olivet Discourse seemed to be wrapped up in the meaning of God's judgment on the old covenant Jews for rejecting the new covenant Messiah. That judgment was embodied in the destruction of the holy city and temple—the symbols of that old order, the destruction of which would historically confirm the spiritual reality that Jesus' sacrifice did away with the temple and its rituals.

The only thing that still seemed to be stuck in the future was the coming of the Son of Man.

Back to the Future

When I looked up other places where Jesus talked about his coming, I began to see that this notion of his coming during the lifetime of his disciples was not in this one lone passage. It was in several passages throughout the New Testament! How had I missed it?

In Matthew 24:13, Jesus linked endurance in faith with the final judgment of the end of the age. And he made this same prediction in Matthew 10:22-23, which uncovers more of the meaning.

In Matthew 10, Jesus told his disciples that he was sending them out to witness to Jews and Gentiles. He warned them that they would be persecuted and that they would be hated by all men for his name's sake, just like in chapter 24. Sure enough, we saw this very thing fulfilled not much later in the book of Acts and the rest of the New Testament. The disciples who became the apostles *were* hated by all because of Christ.

But Jesus added to that prophecy.

> Matthew 10:22–23
> But the one who endures to the end will be saved. [23] When they persecute you in one town, flee to the next, for truly, I say to you, you will not have gone through all the towns of Israel before the Son of Man comes."

---

[1] Kenneth L. Gentry, Jr., *The Divorce of Israel: A Redemptive-Historical Interpretation of Revelation*, (Dallas, GA: Tolle Lege Press, 2016), 54.

So Jesus told his disciples to go through the cities of Israel, which they did indeed do. Remember Acts 1:8? "You will be my witnesses in Jerusalem and in all Judea and Samaria, and to the end of the earth." True to form, we see the disciples in the book of Acts preaching through the towns of Israel, wiping the dust off their feet after being persecuted and then fleeing to the next town.

But then what Jesus said next in chapter 10 completely repudiates the futurist schemes of Christ's coming. He said *to his disciples* that they would not have gone through all the towns of Israel before the Son of Man came! So the Son of Man was coming within their lifetime, not thousands of years later? It is easy to see why literalists turn this passage into figurative reference. They have a preconceived commitment to their eschatology that says the coming of the Son of Man can only be *what they think it can be.* Rather than letting the text speak for itself, a passage addressed to Jesus' own disciples becomes transformed into a warning for some future generation.

What's more, the writer of Hebrews concurred with Jesus' first century interpretation when he wrote the same thing regarding endurance to the final end of the old covenant age.

> Hebrews 10:36–37 (NASB95)
> For you have need of endurance, so that when you have done the will of God, you may receive what was promised. [37] FOR YET IN A VERY LITTLE WHILE, HE WHO IS COMING WILL COME, AND WILL NOT DELAY.

Again, the call is for enduring to the end, connected with the coming of Christ within "a very little while," not "a very long while." The Son of Man was coming before the disciples would finish going through the towns of Israel with the gospel. Not thousands of years from then, but within their own lifetime.

Oh, but that was only warming up. Later, when Jesus stood before the high priest, he made it even clearer that premillennialists and dispensationalists are wrong.

> Matthew 16:27–28
> For the Son of Man is going to come with his angels in the glory of his Father, and then he will repay each person

> according to what he has done. [28] Truly, I say to you, there are some standing here who will not taste death until they see the Son of Man coming in his kingdom."

This is another clear passage about the coming of the Son of Man in all his glory with his angels. Same event as Matthew 24:30-31. Then, as if to answer evangelical futurists, he said that some of those standing right before him would not die before they saw him coming in his kingdom. His coming was within their lifetime, not ours. How is that for a plain reading of the text?

But he didn't stop there. When Jesus was before the high priest, he remained silent until the priest demanded more of him.

> Matthew 26:63–64
> I adjure you by the living God, tell us if you are the Christ, the Son of God. [64] Jesus said to him, "You have said so. But I tell you, from now on you will see the Son of Man seated at the right hand of Power and coming on the clouds of heaven."

Jesus said to the high priest, "You will see," not "they will see," or "a future generation will see." How many more times would Jesus have to say he was coming on the clouds within his generation before I would give in and admit it? In fact, he even added that from then on, the high priest would see Jesus as seated at God's right hand of power, something reserved for deity. This aspect of deity is a very important element of what it means to "come on the clouds." But before I address that, I need to finish the flow of timing made so clear in the New Testament.

At Hand, Near, At the Door

This now makes more sense of the other New Testament authors that seem to be saying that the coming of the Lord was near to them, that it was going to happen to the readers of the original letters in the first century.

> James 5:7–9
> Be patient, therefore, brothers, until the coming of the Lord. … [8] You also, be patient. Establish your hearts, for the coming of the Lord is at hand. [9] Do not grumble against one

another, brothers, so that you may not be judged; behold, the Judge is standing at the door.

2 Thessalonians 2:1–2
Now concerning the coming of our Lord Jesus Christ and our being gathered together to him, we ask you, brothers, [2] not to be quickly shaken in mind or alarmed, either by a spirit or a spoken word, or a letter seeming to be from us, to the effect that the day of the Lord has come.

Philippians 4:4–5
Rejoice in the Lord always; again I will say, rejoice. [5] Let your reasonableness be known to everyone. The Lord is at hand;

Colossians 3:1–4
If then you have been raised with Christ, seek the things that are above, where Christ is, seated at the right hand of God… [4] When Christ who is your life appears, then you also will appear with him in glory.

Modern prophecy pundits have tried to spin these texts by saying that Christ's coming was *imminent*; that is, it could have come at any moment. Even though he would come thousands of years from then, when he did come he would surprise everyone. This is how futurists try to explain away the contradiction of Paul expecting the Lord's coming in his lifetime, while concluding that he never came. But that is not taking the text literally. The text does not say he could come *at any moment* for millennia to come, but that he was "at hand" for those first century believers. This phrase "at hand" is used throughout the Gospels to mean within their lifetime (Matt 26:18; 26:45-46; Luke 21:20; John 2:13; 6:4; 7:2; 7:6; 11:55),[2] not thousands of years later, which would make the phrase "at hand" meaningless. In fact, Jesus used this same "at hand" in Matthew 24:32 of the Olivet Discourse when he said that his coming could be compared to a fig tree with leaves that predicts the summer is "near" (same Greek word). A summer for a fig tree is

---

[2] Gary DeMar, *Left Behind: Separating Fact from Fiction* (Powder Springs, GA: American Vision, 2009), 203–204.

not thousands of weeks away; it is a few weeks away. *Near* means near; *at hand* means within the lifetime of the hearers. It is never used to mean far or many years beyond the lifetime of the hearers.

The book of Revelation repeatedly explains that its end times events would "shortly take place" (1:1, 22:6), that "the time is near" (1:3), that Jesus and those events were "coming quickly" (2:16; 3:11; 11:14; 22:7; 22:12; 22:20). "Near," "quickly," and "at hand" cannot mean thousands of years from now. That would make the words nonsense.

Although futurists try to redefine "near" to mean thousands of years from New Testament times, they will admit that when they use the words "near" and "soon," they mean within their own lifetimes. They will say "The end is near," "the Day of the Lord is at hand," and "Jesus is coming soon." And what do they mean? They mean that they believe Jesus is coming within their own generation.

And that is exactly what the Bible authors meant as well when they wrote "near," "at hand," and "soon." They meant what Jesus meant when he said "this generation." They meant *within their lifetime*.

So why don't we have a biblical or historical document of this massive, intrusive coming of Christ on the clouds? Surely, if that had happened, there would be a record of it.

There is. We just don't see it because we don't think as the ancient Hebrews did; so we don't catch it when we read their writings.

The first clue to me that something was wrong about the way we interpret Christ's coming was in Paul's letter to the Thessalonians, already quoted above.

> Thessalonians 2:1–2
> Now concerning the coming of our Lord Jesus Christ and our being gathered together to him, we ask you, brothers, [2] not to be quickly shaken in mind or alarmed, either by a spirit or a spoken word, or a letter seeming to be from us, to the effect that the day of the Lord has come.

Paul was telling them not to believe others who said that the Lord had already come. Wait a minute, I thought. If Christ's coming would be massive, worldwide, and the end of time, how is it that Paul would be worried about the Thessalonians mistakenly thinking that it had already come? If Paul had defined the coming of Christ as the end of history and the worldwide final judgment, he would not be worried that someone might deceive the Thessalonians about the day of the Lord having already come. They would laugh such claims out of the city. There is only one way that there could be such a misunderstanding of missing Christ's coming: if Paul did not define it as a massive, worldwide, end of history, and final judgment, but rather as something else, something more local and limited.

A Sign in Heaven or the Son of Man in Heaven?

> Matthew 24:30–31
> Then will appear in heaven the sign of the Son of Man, and then all the tribes of the earth will mourn, and they will see the Son of Man coming on the clouds of heaven with power and great glory. [31] And he will send out his angels with a loud trumpet call, and they will gather his elect from the four winds, from one end of heaven to the other.

The first problem with understanding this verse about Christ's coming is the grammar. Unfortunately, the Greek grammar is not clear. This translation reads that a sign in the sky or "heaven" will appear, indicating the Son of Man. However, it is just as grammatically correct, and actually makes more sense, for the text to be translated "and then will appear, the sign of the Son of Man in heaven," as the KJV, NIV, RSV, and others translate it. There is no sign in heaven (or the sky) that Jesus is coming; there is a sign that Jesus is in heaven.

This makes more sense with other scriptures where Jesus is described as being in heaven at the right hand of God, endowed with his power.

> Matthew 26:64
> Jesus said to him, "You have said so. But I tell you, <u>from now on you will see the Son of Man seated at the right hand of Power and coming on the clouds of heaven."</u>

> Acts 7:55–56
> But [Stephen], full of the Holy Spirit, gazed into heaven and saw the glory of God, and Jesus standing <u>at the right hand of</u>

God. [56] And he said, "Behold, I see the heavens opened, and the Son of Man standing at the right hand of God."

Colossians 3:1
If then you have been raised with Christ, seek the things that are above, where Christ is, seated at the right hand of God.

Hebrews 1:3
He is the radiance of the glory of God and the exact imprint of his nature, and he upholds the universe by the word of his power. After making purification for sins, he sat down at the right hand of the Majesty on high.

Hebrews 8:1
Now the point in what we are saying is this: we have such a high priest, one who is seated at the right hand of the throne of the Majesty in heaven,

Hebrews 10:12–13
But when Christ had offered for all time a single sacrifice for sins, he sat down at the right hand of God, [13] waiting from that time until his enemies should be made a footstool for his feet.

1 Peter 3:21–22
Jesus Christ, [22] who has gone into heaven and is at the right hand of God, with angels, authorities, and powers having been subjected to him.

Ephesians 1:20–22
that he worked in Christ when he raised him from the dead and seated him at his right hand in the heavenly places, [21] far above all rule and authority and power and dominion, and above every name that is named, not only in this age but also in the one to come. [22] And he put all things under his feet.

Romans 8:34
Who is to condemn? Christ Jesus is the one who died—more than that, who was raised—who is at the right hand of God, who indeed is interceding for us.

The notion of Christ at the right hand of God in heaven permeates the New Testament. But I want you to notice something else consistently in all these passages. Notice how that right hand represents God's power and authority over all powers and authorities, both earthly and heavenly. That power is ultimately deity as we will see shortly. But again, this makes sense with Jesus' judgment on the Jews who rejected his authority as Messiah. He was saying that the destruction of their entire covenantal system would be the final sign of the messianic covenantal authority of Christ that they rejected. How do I know he was still referencing the Jews in his judgment and not the entire world at the end of time? Because he said so in the very next verse.

The Tribes of the Land

We have seen over and over again that our bias can blind us to the context of the original writers and readers of the ancient biblical text. Now we run into another example of that bias that even exists in the translations of the Bible! After the sign of the Son of Man in heaven we read,

Matthew 24:30
[T]hen all the tribes of the earth will mourn, and they will see the Son of Man coming on the clouds of heaven with power and great glory.

Here is a phrase that seems clearly to indicate a worldwide coming and judgment. "All the tribes of the earth" can only mean everyone around the globe, right?

Wrong. The Greek word translated "earth" here is *ge*, which is most often translated as "land." It either refers to terra firma, the ground we stand on, the dirt, or the empire, as we saw earlier. But for the Jewish audience, "the land" had a specific meaning that the word "earth" does not reveal, and that meaning is the land of Israel.

Jesus was saying that the tribes of *the land of Israel* will mourn when they see the proof of his messiahship in heaven: the destruction of their temple. And this is exactly what was prophesied in the Old Testament and fulfilled in the first century.

> Zechariah 12:10
> And I will pour out on the house of David and the inhabitants of Jerusalem a spirit of grace and pleas for mercy, so that, when they look on me, on him whom they have pierced, they shall mourn for him, as one mourns for an only child, and weep bitterly over him, as one weeps over a firstborn.

We already established in chapter 7 that the Jews of the first century were considered guilty by God and the apostles of rejecting Messiah and killing him by crucifixion ("whom they have pierced"). The New Testament says that this Scripture of "looking on him whom they have pierced" is fulfilled in the crucifixion and in the later destruction of Jerusalem.

> John 19:36–37
> For these things took place that the Scripture might be fulfilled:…"They will look on him whom they have pierced."

> Revelation 1:7
> Behold, he is coming with the clouds, and every eye will see him, even those who pierced him, and all tribes of the earth [land] will wail on account of him.

The book of Revelation references *ge* quite a bit, as in this passage. You can easily see how deeply misunderstood Revelation has become by mistranslating the word as "earth" instead of "land," which makes people misread it as "globe" instead of "land of Israel." Reread Revelation now with this awareness and you'll see a real change in the meaning.

But suffice it to say that Jesus coming in judgment upon Jerusalem was like saying, "Then you'll be sorry you crucified me."

Coming on the Clouds of Heaven

Now we come to the most amazing part of the prophecy. I had always understood "coming on the clouds" as being an obvious, literal allusion to

Jesus floating in on clouds in the sky in a climactic ending to history. What else could it mean? This seemed to be the biggest obstacle to surmount in understanding the Olivet Discourse as a prophecy of the first century coming of Christ at the end of the old covenant age.

Then I was shown in the Old Testament the very clear precedent of this metaphor. With a new understanding of the ancient Jewish mindset and how they interpreted these words, I began to see it as the very opposite of the wooden, literalistic event I used to see it as. Let me show you what changed my mind, and I'm sure it will begin to change yours.

"Coming on the clouds" is used throughout the Old Testament as a figurative storm reference to God's judging presence upon a city, nation, or people. Clouds and storm are both metaphors for deity and for local judgment. Here is a brief survey of the instances.

When God judged the city of Nineveh in the days of Nahum the prophet…

> Nahum 1:2–3
> The LORD takes vengeance on his adversaries and keeps wrath for his enemies. [3]…His way is in whirlwind and storm, and the clouds are the dust of his feet.

When God delivered David and judged Saul…

> Psalm 18:9–11
> He bowed the heavens and came down; thick darkness was under his feet. [10] He rode on a cherub and flew; he came swiftly on the wings of the wind. [11] He made darkness his covering, his canopy around him, thick clouds dark with water.

When God judged Egypt in the days of Ezekiel, he said,

> Ezekiel 30:3–4
> For the day is near, the day of the LORD is near; it will be a day of clouds… [4] A sword shall come upon Egypt.

In 721 B.C., Isaiah prophesied judgment against Egypt that occurred by about 701 B.C.

> Isaiah 19:1
> An oracle concerning Egypt. Behold, the LORD is riding on a swift cloud and comes to Egypt;

When God judged Assyria in 701 B.C. he described his anger. ..

> Isaiah 30:30
> And the Lord will cause his majestic voice to be heard and the descending blow of his arm to be seen, in furious anger and a flame of devouring fire, with a cloudburst and storm and hailstones.

Remember that passage in Joel about the last days that Peter said was being fulfilled in his day? You guessed it, more clouds of judgment.

> Joel 2:1–2
> [F]or the day of the LORD is coming; it is near, [2] a day of darkness and gloom, a day of clouds and thick darkness!

These are all local and limited judgments upon cities, nations, or peoples, and they all use the imagery of God coming on the clouds with the storm of judgment. This was a common ancient image of God's judgment. Did God literally come floating in on clouds in the sky to Nineveh, Saul, or Egypt? Of course not. Clouds and storm were figurative expressions, literary signs of his spiritual presence in the local and limited judgments upon those nations and cities. So, Jesus coming on the clouds of heaven in power and glory was an obvious figurative expression of Jesus' presence in the judgment upon Jerusalem, the sign of his power and the glory of the new covenant.

But there is one more thing. In each of these cases, God used a different nation or people as his tool to perform the judgment. In other words, the pagan people carried out God's will; they represented him spiritually.

God used Babylon to judge Assyria in Nahum.[3] God used Babylon to judge Egypt in Ezekiel 30:10. God used the Egyptians against themselves

---

[3] "When Nabopolassar (626–605 B.C.), the conqueror of Nineveh, drove the Assyrians from Babylonia, he proclaimed, "The Assyrian who had ruled Akkad [Babylonia] … and had, with his heavy yoke, oppressed the inhabitants of the country … I removed them from Akkad and caused [the Babylonians] to throw off their yoke." John H Walton, Zondervan Illustrated Bible Backgrounds Commentary (Old Testament): *The Minor Prophets, Job, Psalms, Proverbs, Ecclesiastes, Song of Songs*, vol. 5 (Grand Rapids, MI: Zondervan, 2009), 154.

(Isa 19:2) as well as the Assyrians to judge Egypt (Isa 19:4).[4] And so, God would use the Romans to be his hand of judgment upon Israel in A.D. 70 when they destroyed the city and temple. God often used pagan forces of destruction to humble his people. But fear not, God then judged those pagans for their evil as well! God promised he would do this to the Romans after their desolation.

> Daniel 9:27
> And on the wing of abominations shall come one who makes desolate, until the decreed end is poured out on the desolator.

The Roman empire eventually did fall. A good historical argument has been made that though the barbarians ultimately invaded and overthrew Rome, its power first became crippled within, due to the growth of Christianity that subverted pagan devotion to the idolatrous authority of Caesar.

Where Have I Seen This Before?

A final clincher on the description of Christ's coming on the clouds is in the book of Daniel. It is no coincidence that Jesus quoted Daniel's abomination of desolation and then described himself as the Son of Man coming on the clouds, prophesied by Daniel as well. And if we look at it, we'll see that it reinforces everything I've been writing.

> Daniel 7:13–14
> I saw in the night visions, and behold, with the clouds of heaven there came one like a son of man, and he came to the Ancient of Days and was presented before him. [14] And to him was given dominion and glory and a kingdom, that all peoples, nations, and languages should serve him; his dominion is an everlasting dominion, which shall not pass away, and his kingdom one that shall not be destroyed.

---

[4] "A hand that Israel would also find harsh is that of the Assyrians, who could also be meant here." John H Walton, *Zondervan Illustrated Bible Backgrounds Commentary (Old Testament): Isaiah, Jeremiah, Lamentations, Ezekiel, Daniel*, vol. 4 (Grand Rapids, MI: Zondervan, 2009), 84–85.

Remember all those passages you read earlier about Jesus being at the right hand of God to receive the kingdom and power and authority? Those were all affirmations of this same passage in Daniel. The right hand of God is the place of omnipotent power. It is the ultimate position of authority over all. Coming on the clouds is an expression of supreme deity and absolute power.

> Hebrews 10:12–13
> But when Christ had offered for all time a single sacrifice for sins, he sat down at the right hand of God, [13] waiting from that time until his enemies should be made a footstool for his feet.

As in Daniel 7, the one at God's right hand receives dominion and authority over all peoples, nations, and languages that they should serve him. This Son of Man in Daniel 2 and 7 is the Messiah of the new covenant, the kingdom of God, and the Son of Man in Matthew 24. And Daniel 7 was not about the second coming of Christ, it was about his first coming. Daniel 7 was fulfilled at Jesus' ascension around A.D. 30, as Ephesians explains.

> Ephesians 1:20–22
> [He] worked in Christ when he raised him from the dead and seated him at his right hand in the heavenly places, [21] far above all rule and authority and power and dominion, and above every name that is named, not only in this age but also in the one to come. [22] And he put all things under his feet.

But notice something else: there are those clouds of heaven again. Clouds, not merely of deity but of judgment over the nations. For this cornerstone "cut without hands" would "break in pieces all these kingdoms and bring them to an end, and it shall stand forever" (Dan 2:44). Those kingdoms that were in fact7 broken to pieces were Babylon, Medo-Persia, Greece, and *Rome*. Ancient Rome that crucified Messiah—the fourth world kingdom of Daniel 2:40—would fall and be crushed by the cornerstone of Messiah.

But look closer and you will see that the Son of Man coming on the clouds was not *coming down to earth* from the sky, but rather was *coming up* to the throne of God in heaven to sit at God's right hand. Jesus wasn't coming down to earth in Matthew 24:30. The destruction of the city and temple were a sign that Jesus was the messianic Son of Man and that he had come up to the right hand of God. It was the proof to the Jews that the Roman destruction of their city and temple was Jesus/God's judgment because they had rejected the Messiah. It was the sign that the Son of Man was in heaven at the right hand of God with messianic power and glory!

> Matthew 26:63–64
> The high priest said to him, "I adjure you by the living God, tell us if you are the Christ, the Son of God." [64] Jesus said to him, "You have said so. But I tell you, from now on you will see the Son of Man seated at the right hand of Power and coming on the clouds of heaven."

But if this is true, if this coming of the Son of Man is not the end of the world, then what in the world did he mean by the angels gathering the elect? I always thought that was either the rapture or the resurrection.

Angels Gathering the Elect

After Jesus came in judgment upon Jerusalem and confirmed his authority at the right hand of God by destroying the old covenant symbols for good, he then sent out his angels for a task.

> Matthew 24:31
> And he will send out his angels with a loud trumpet call, and they will gather his elect from the four winds, from one end of heaven to the other.

By now, it will be no surprise to discover that our modern evangelical assumptions and translations are inaccurate.

The Greek word for "angel," *angelos* (or *angelous/angelon*), does not always mean a divine being from heaven. In fact, its most primary meaning is "messenger." Yes, those messengers are often divine beings from heaven in the Bible. But not always. Sometimes, they are human!

John the Baptist was an angel of God.

> Matthew 11:10
> This is he of whom it is written, "Behold, I send my messenger [*angelos*] before your face, who will prepare your way before you."

John the Baptist's disciples were called John's angels.

> Luke 7:24
> When John's messengers [*angelon*] had gone, Jesus began to speak to the crowds concerning John: "What did you go out into the wilderness to see? A reed shaken by the wind?

The Jewish spies who snuck into Jericho were called angels.

> James 2:25
> And in the same way was not also Rahab the prostitute justified by works when she received the messengers [*angelous*] and sent them out by another way?

And Jesus' own disciples were called angels.

> Luke 9:52
> And he sent messengers [*angelous*] ahead of him, who went and entered a village of the Samaritans, to make preparations for him.

Ken Gentry makes a strong biblical argument in his Revelation commentary that the "angels" of the seven churches in Revelation may actually have been the human Christian messengers of the letter to the congregation, lectors who would read the text to the church body, since they didn't have their own Bibles.[5]

Think about it: we Christians are the messengers of the gospel to the world, aren't we? In that sense, we are God's *angelous*, his angels. We bring the message of the gospel to the four winds of the earth, just as he commanded (Acts 1:8). And God has used the gospel as the means to gather his elect into his kingdom. Whether you believe they are elect first and then

---

[5] Kenneth L. Gentry, Jr., "Part One: In The Spirit On Patmos, Rev 1:9–3:22, D. Explication (1:19–20)," *The Divorce of Israel: A Redemptive-Historical Interpretation of Revelation*, (Dallas, GA: Tolle Lege Press, 2017), unpublished.

believe, or they first believe and are then elect, the end remains the same: they are gathered into God's kingdom through the proclamation of the gospel. The loud trumpet is reminiscent of the shofar trumpet in the temple that would call the Jews to worship, or it could call them to war. Now that the physical temple would be destroyed, this trumpet call is an obvious figurative expression of the call to preach the gospel to the lost.

And historically speaking, this is exactly what happened after Jesus came in judgment upon Jerusalem, destroyed the temple, and led the Jews into captivity; the Christians escaped and were dispersed to spread the gospel to all nations, a gospel that gathered together the children of God from all nations.

> John 11:51
> Being high priest that year he prophesied that Jesus would die for the nation, [52] and not for the nation only, but also to gather into one the children of God who are scattered abroad."

As we see in this and other New Testament passages, the growth of the Church is the fulfillment of the promise for God's people to be brought out of exile from the nations (Acts 2; Romans 10, quoting Isaiah 52 and 53 about the return from exile). As New Testament scholar N.T. Wright explains,

> The end of this exile, and the real 'return', are not now future events to be experienced in terms of a cleansed Land, a rebuilt Temple, an intensified Torah. The exile came to its cataclysmic end when Jesus, Israel's representative Messiah, died outside the walls of Jerusalem, bearing the curse, which consisted of exile at the hands of the pagans, to its utmost limit. The return from exile began when Jesus, again as the representative Messiah, emerged from the tomb three days later.[6]

There is one last important piece that can easily be missed in the English translation with our modern Western viewpoint. That Greek word for "gather" that John used for gathering the children of God (11:51) is the

---

[6] N. T. Wright, *The New Testament and the People of God*, Christian Origins and the Question of God (London: Society for Promoting Christian Knowledge, 1992), 406.

word *synagogue*. That should of course ring bells in the reader's memory. "Synagogue" is the word for the gathering of the Jews in each city. A similar Greek word is used for the angels "gathering" the elect in Matthew 24:31: *episynago* (an expansion of *synagogue*).

So the "gathering" of the elect by angels is not a miraculous rapture or resurrection, but rather the congregational assembly of God's people. It refers to God building his "church" (*ekklesia*: "assembly"), the new "assembly" of God's people, by drawing them from every nation into the kingdom through the call of the gospel (Matt 23:37; Acts 2; John 6:44; 10:16; Rom 10:17). And, lo and behold, this is exactly what God prophesied in the Old Testament (LXX).

> Deuteronomy 30:3-4
> And the Lord shall heal your sins, and he will show mercy to you, and he will gather (*synagogue*) you again from all the nations into which the Lord scattered you there. [4]If your dispersion should be from one end of heaven as far as the other end of heaven, from that place the Lord your God will gather (*synagogue*) you and from that place the Lord your God will take you.[7]

In conclusion, I will quote Revelation scholar Kenneth Gentry as a fitting summary of what the judgment-coming of Christ upon Jerusalem is all about in these passages we have been exploring. Though the following quote is about the book of Revelation, Gentry also argues that this applies to Christ's statements in Matthew 23-24:

> Christ's judgment-coming effects several dramatic results: it brings God's wrath upon the Jews for rejecting their Messiah (Mt 21:33–44; 23:37–38; Ac 2:36); it concludes the anticipatory old covenant era (Heb 1:1; 12:18– 29) which in the first century is "becoming obsolete and growing old" and is "ready to vanish away" (Heb 8:13; cp. Gal 3:23–25); it finally and forever closes down the typological sacrificial

---

[7] Rick Brannan et al., eds., *The Lexham English Septuagint* (Bellingham, WA: Lexham Press, 2012), Dt 30:3–5.

> system, reorienting the worship of God (Jn 4:21; Heb 9–10); it vindicates Christ's followers against their first enemies (Mt 10:16–23; 23:24–24:2; 1Th 2:14–17; Rev 6:9–11); and it effectively universalizes the Christian faith by freeing it from all Jewish constraints (Mt 28:18–20; Mk 2:21–22; Ac 15:10–11; Eph 2:12–22).[8]

Is There No Return of Christ in Our Future?

Wow! I never thought I would ever get to the point where I would see the coming of Christ in Matthew 24 as a figurative judgment coming in the armies of pagan Rome. But there I was; I could not deny it from the text. Everything was fulfilled historically. And I had the biblical documentation. Now the problem was that all my other assumptions became unstable and shaky. Did this mean Christ was not returning in my future? Was his coming in the first century the only coming of Christ spoken of in other passages? I mean, if Christ already came, what would we have to look forward to? I felt insecure, as if my whole understanding of God and the future was up in the air.

It is an uncomfortable place to be. But isn't it better to follow the truth wherever it leads—even if that becomes scary—than to stay safe, comfortable and wrong? Fear not; the truth leads to a physical return of Christ in our future, a general physical resurrection of the dead, a final judgment, and to the next chapter.

---

[8] Kenneth L. Gentry, Jr., *The Divorce of Israel: A Redemptive-Historical Interpretation of Revelation*, (Dallas, GA: Tolle Lege Press, 2016), 48-49

Chapter 14
The Return of Christ

So there I was, having just biblically discovered that the "coming of the Son of Man" is not necessarily a phrase referring only to a physical return of Christ as I had been erroneously taught. God "comes" in many different ways in the Scriptures, and the most common way was to come spiritually in judgment upon a city or nation *in and through* pagan rulers and their armies. This was what happened in A.D. 70. Jesus came in judgment upon Israel in the Roman armies of the abominable Titus. My next thought was that this completely eliminated a physical return of Christ, and with it, other important doctrinal beliefs. But that next thought was not a Scriptural one. I studied the issue more and ultimately concluded that there is still a physical return of Christ in our future. How could that be? Didn't I just wipe out the claims to Christ coming in the future by wiping it out of Matthew 24?

Not necessarily. Don't forget: just because you've discovered that *one* or more passages do not teach the physical return of Christ does not mean *no other passages* do. You can believe in the physical return of Christ even if Matthew 24 doesn't teach it—if other passages do teach it.

I have found out that there are different preterist interpretations of Christ's coming. Full preterists or hyperpreterists do believe that every passage in the New Testament that talks of Christ's coming refers to the judgment of A.D. 70. But partial preterists or orthodox preterists believe that some passages still teach a physical coming of Christ in our future (for example, 1 Cor 15), depending on the context. But how could this be? Isn't it a contradiction to say that Jesus already came in the first century, but he is coming again?

Not if you follow the Bible. So, let's follow the Bible.

God Comes to Us in Many Different Ways

I already learned that God came in judgment multiple times upon multiple cities or nations in the history of the Old Testament. So the precedent was already set. This thinking already pervaded the Hebrew worldview.

But I discovered that the New Testament also talks of Jesus coming in multiple, different ways as well.

First, and most explicitly, Jesus said that his judgment upon the Jews for rejecting him was a coming that involved the establishment of the new covenant.

> Mark 12:9–10
> What will the owner of the vineyard do? He will come and destroy the tenants and give the vineyard to others.

Technically, the owner in this parable is God the Father who sent his Son. But as Matthew 1:23 indicates, Jesus is "God with us." So as God the Son, his incarnational coming is God coming to us (Luke 19:44).

But coming in judgment is not the only kind of Christ's coming that we read about in the New Testament. He also comes in peace. Jesus said that he would come to his people, Christians, in the Holy Spirit. First, he came to the disciples after his death; and, logically, that coming extends to every Christian who believes.

> John 14:18
> I will not leave you as orphans; I will come to you.

> John 14:28
> You heard me say to you, "I am going away, and I will come to you."

Jesus also said he would come to Christians in fellowship. This is a coming of Christ that is multiplied as many times as there are Christians willing to open their doors to him.

> Revelation 3:20
> Behold, I stand at the door and knock. If anyone hears my voice and opens the door, I will come in to him and eat with him, and he with me.

Daniel spoke of the Son of Man coming on the clouds of heaven, not in our distant future, but in our past when he was seated at the right hand of God during his ascension.

Daniel 7:13–14
Behold, with the clouds of heaven there came one like a son of man, and he came to the Ancient of Days and was presented before him. [14] And to him was given dominion and glory and a kingdom.

Remember, Jesus was seated at God's right hand and given all power and authority at his ascension, shortly after his resurrection. So that was one coming, a coming up (ascension) to God's throne to receive all power and dominion at the right hand of God (Eph 1:19-22).

The book of Revelation is about the big picture of God's judgment, but it speaks of many different comings of Christ. Specifically, when Jesus gave a word to the seven churches of Asia Minor, he gave them a blessing and a warning. And his warnings involved him coming to those cities with specific judgment if they did not repent for their sins.

Revelation 2:5 (to the church of Ephesus)
Remember therefore from where you have fallen; repent, and do the works you did at first. If not, I will come to you and remove your lampstand from its place, unless you repent.

Revelation 2:16 (to the church of Pergamum)
Therefore repent. If not, I will come to you soon and war against them with the sword of my mouth.

Revelation 2:25–26 (to the church of Thyatira)
Only hold fast what you have until I come. [26] The one who conquers and who keeps my works until the end, to him I will give authority over the nations.

Revelation 3:3 (to the church of Sardis)
Remember, then, what you received and heard. Keep it, and repent. If you will not wake up, I will come like a thief, and you will not know at what hour I will come against you.

Revelation 3:11–12 (to the church of Philadelphia)
I am coming soon. Hold fast what you have, so that no one may seize your crown.

Notice that these various comings of Christ to multiple cities in Revelation were all conditional. Jesus' coming to each city was based on potential judgment; but if they repented they wouldn't be judged. So the notion of Christ or God coming to visit judgment upon cities, be they pagan, Jewish or Christian, was a common understanding of the ancient Hebrew mind. Jesus could and did come in different ways at different times. Christ's various spiritual comings in judgment to Jerusalem, Babylon, Egypt and others in the Old Testament, or to Jerusalem in A.D. 70, does not necessarily preclude a physical coming at the end of history for the resurrection and final judgment.

The problem is that there is much written about Christ's judgment coming upon Israel in the New Testament because it was about to be fulfilled in their generation. They knew that event was coming and so it was on the forefront of their minds and in the New Testament writings. The apostles were trying to encourage the persecuted Christians to endure and to prepare for the massive violence about to descend upon Jerusalem and the land of Israel that would lead to the victory of the Gospel spreading out upon the earth. Sometimes the writers then used that localized judgment as yet another typological herald pointing to the universal judgment. Thus it is not always easy for the casual Bible reader to interpret the difference between the passages of localized judgment in their day, and Christ's universal judgment at the end of history. After all, the terminology used is similar. I don't have the space to exegete this fully since that is not the main purpose of this book, so I will just address the strongest text that affirms the basic orthodox doctrine of the return of Christ, the general resurrection and the final judgment.

1 Corinthians 15

While there are passages that refer to a future return of Christ and general resurrection (John 5:25-29; Phil 3:10, 20-21), 1 Corinthians 15 is the one passage that I would like to take a look at very briefly. In the first half of the chapter, Paul talks about the importance of the historical physical resurrection of Christ to the truth and power of the Gospel to save. He explains that Christ's resurrection prefigures our own resurrection at his coming.

> 1 Corinthians 15:20–26
> But in fact Christ has been raised from the dead, the firstfruits of those who have fallen asleep. [21] For as by a man came

> death, by a man has come also the resurrection of the dead. [22] For as in Adam all die, so also in Christ shall all be made alive. [23] But each in his own order: Christ the firstfruits, then at his coming those who belong to Christ. [24] Then comes the end, when he delivers the kingdom to God the Father after destroying every rule and every authority and power. [25] For he must reign until he has put all his enemies under his feet. [26] The last enemy to be destroyed is death.

I don't think that his "coming" or "the end" here is Christ's judgment coming upon Jerusalem or Matthew's "end of the age" as we saw earlier. I think this is referring to Christ's physical return at the end of history. The end of the Old Testament age is not the only end that Bible prophecy talks about. First, a physical resurrection of the dead has not occurred. And we will see in a moment that it is a physical resurrection, not a spiritual resurrection. Secondly, though Christ was given all rule and authority at his resurrection and ascension, and now reigns from God's right hand (Eph 1:20-23), this is only the legally inaugurated authority. As the writer of Hebrews explains, we will see the full working out and consummation of that authority progressively in history as more and more people are put under his feet through salvation.

> Hebrews 2:7–9
> You have crowned [Jesus] with glory and honor, [8] putting everything in subjection under his feet." Now in putting everything in subjection to him, he left nothing outside his control. At present, we do not yet see everything in subjection to him. [9] But we see him who for a little while was made lower than the angels, namely Jesus, crowned with glory and honor because of the suffering of death.

After the kingdom of God has grown to be a mountain that fills the earth (Dan 2:35, 44-45), or the mustard seed that has grown to be the biggest tree on the garden of the earth (Matt 13:31-32), then Jesus will hand the kingdom over to God. Not until then. Only then will death be defeated with the resurrection of our glorified bodies made immortal.

Full preterists believe that 1 Corinthians 15 refers to the A.D. 70 coming and that the resurrection spoken of is a spiritual resurrection. It is one of two things: a metaphor of a person dying and going to heaven with a purely spiritual body without physicality or a metaphor for the collective Church or body of Christ being raised up or gathered together. I do not believe these interpretations for a couple reasons. First, Paul likens our future resurrection to the same exact form and nature as Christ's resurrection, which was clearly a physical resurrection, not a mere spiritual resurrection or a spirit body without flesh. Secondly, Paul then explains what he means by resurrection body versus our natural body in verses 35-49. Though there is plenty of theological debate on this, I see the text comparing our resurrected bodies with our current natural bodies not as spiritual versus physical, but as immortal and perfected physical bodies versus mortal sin-tainted flesh that we currently have under the curse of death.

Then comes the clincher. Paul clarifies his point by indicating that he is not talking about spiritual versus physical, but rather imperishable versus perishable. He says that "This mortal body must put on immortality" (v. 53), not that this mortal body should put off its physicality. This mortal body is our current physical body. Our spirit will not slough off our flesh, but rather, our physical body will become glorified and immortal—just like Jesus' physically immortal body (1Jn 3:2). That is a future resurrection that occurs when Christ physically returns for a final judgment of all mankind. And *that* is for another book.

I am by no means suggesting that this is a detailed argument that will satisfy the exegetical concerns of full preterists, but my goal was only to comfort other millennialists with the truth that they don't have to give up the return of Christ just because they learn that sometimes "coming" in the Bible refers to Christ's judgment coming in A.D. 70. For those who want more in depth scholarly explanation of resurrection in 1 Corinthians, I highly recommend N.T. Wright's magisterial *The Resurrection of the Son of God.*[1] For an excellent book addressing the problems of full preterism I

[1] N. T. Wright, *The Resurrection of the Son of God, Christian Origins and the Question of God* (London: Society for Promoting Christian Knowledge, 2003), 312-361.

recommend Joel McDurmon's *We Shall All Be Changed: A Future Bodily Resurrection Of The Saints.*[2]

Now, let's get back to Matthew 24.

[2] Joel McDurmon's *We Shall All Be Changed: A Future Bodily Resurrection Of The Saints* (GA: American Vision, 2012). Also read: Samuel M. Frost, *Why I Left Full Preterism* (Powder Springs, GA: American Vision). Both books can be ordered from: http://americanvision.org. Also, read Kenneth L. Gentry Jr., *Have We Missed The Second Coming?: A Critique of the Hyper-preterist Error* (Fountain Inn, SC: Victorious Hope Publishing, 2016) Order at: http://www.kennethgentry.com.

Chapter 15
The Day and the Hour

"No one knows the day or the hour!" This terminology is often trumpeted over and over by those futurist prophecy pundits who nevertheless make predictions of the day and the hour, couched in the language of "maybe" and "possibly" and other "day and hour" surrogates. They think that if they couch their speculation in questions such as "Could this be what the prophet foretold?" and "Is this the meaning of the prophecy?" that they remain unaccountable for their obvious predictions. They act as if qualifying all their forecasting that we are in the last days before Christ's return protects them from the charge of false prophesying.

Sadly, it does not. When Hal Lindsey said that the 1970s were the last generation and would see the return of Christ, he thought that predicting Christ's coming to that *generation* was not the same as predicting "the day or the hour." But it really was the same thing. And that generation is long past. When Edgar Whisenant predicted that Christ would come in 1988, he claimed he was predicting the *year*, not the *day or the hour,* as if that let him off the hook. But it doesn't. Lucky for these prophecy pundits and their current counterparts that we are not living under the Old Testament Law, because they would be stoned to death for being false prophets. Unlucky for the rest of us that people still follow after these and many other futurists, even after so many failed predictions and changes of prophecies that it makes your head spin.

Remember at the very beginning of this journey when I mentioned that Jesus' prophecies in the Olivet discourse were bookended with the phrase that all these things would come upon his generation? We are now at the other book end of that sermon where he reiterated in Matthew 24:34 that "this generation will not pass away until all these things take place." We have seen how *all these things* included false christs, wars and rumors of wars, famines, earthquakes, the abomination of desolation, the great tribulation, the sun and moon being darkened, the stars falling from heaven, and, yes, even the coming of the Son of Man with power and glory. All these things occurred within the generation of those who were listening to Jesus preach. It culminated in the destruction of the holy city and temple as God's final, historical affirmation of the end of the old covenant and the final establishment of the new covenant with his people, the church of Jesus Christ.

This last section of the chapter deals with a fourfold warning that blends into parables of warning in chapter 25. The four images that Jesus evoked are the fig tree, the days of Noah, a thief in the night, and the wise and wicked servants. All four of these images reinforced the nearness and seriousness of the coming judgment upon Israel and the need to prepare.

The Fig Tree

The fig tree as a symbol for Israel becoming a modern nation has been a popular misinterpretation of this passage by dispensationalists and other futurists. I deconstruct this myth in my booklet *Israel in Bible Prophecy: The New Testament Fulfillment of the Promise to Abraham*. (The reader can get that booklet at online booksellers where they purchased this book).

The problem with modern interpretation of images like this is that it tends to invest too much of its own context into the meaning of an image or parable. Images and parables are usually used to make one or two main points for emphasis, but modern interpreters tend to allegorize every element of the analogy well beyond the stated intent.

It's much more simple than prophecy pundits would like you to think.

Jesus told us exactly the single intent of the fig tree image: the nearness of his predictions.

> Matthew 24:32
> From the fig tree learn its lesson: as soon as its branch becomes tender and puts out its leaves, you know that summer is near.

That's it. Simple and straightforward. No secret meaning. No symbolism of Israel. Just a metaphor for the nearness of events. And then he defined exactly what nearness meant in the very next verse.

> Matthew 24:33–34
> So also, when you see all these things, you know that he is near, at the very gates. [34] Truly, I say to you, this generation will not pass away until all these things take place.

Jesus reiterated that his coming was near, within the generation of those he was speaking to. And of course, *all these things* did happen within that generation, by A.D. 70. To import anything beyond Jesus' own stated explanation is to twist the text for your own predetermined eschatological agenda.

As in the Days of Noah

Jesus' next image of warning was "the days of Noah." And he told us once again exactly the meaning of his image: no one will know the day or hour of his coming. The point was that if his hearers did not repent and prepare for the judgment coming, they would be caught by surprise and caught up in the judgment, just like those in the days of Noah who did not listen to the warnings.

> Matthew 24:36–39
> But concerning that day and hour no one knows, not even the angels of heaven, nor the Son, but the Father only. [37] For as were the days of Noah, so will be the coming of the Son of Man. [38] For as in those days before the flood they were eating and drinking, marrying and giving in marriage, until the day when Noah entered the ark, [39] and they were unaware until the flood came and swept them all away, so will be the coming of the Son of Man.

Many end times researchers and prophecy pundits tend to read into this image far more than Jesus intended. They read, "As were the days of Noah," and then they stop reading, *jump completely out of that context* back to the Genesis 6 account, and read everything about the days of Noah into the present. They conclude that the same things that happened back then are going to happen before Christ's coming. They read about the divine angelic beings, the sons of God, "taking wives" of the daughters of men. These women then birthed hybrid giant offspring called Nephilim, who were the disastrous result of that unholy union that led toward the judgment of the flood. They then make claims that the Nephilim will return before Christ does, or that modern genetic splicing is the new Nephilim hybrid, or other such science fiction speculations.

Some Christians do not believe that Genesis 6 talks about Nephilim hybrid giants and supernatural sons of God, but I do. I wrote an entire book explaining its theological significance in the biblical storyline, *When Giants Were Upon the Earth: The Watchers, The Nephilim and the Biblical Cosmic War of the Seed*. However, I have to say that there is absolutely no biblical warrant for importing the Nephilim and sons of God from the primeval days into Jesus' words. There is no warrant for concluding that Jesus was predicting a return of the Nephilim. Jesus *explicitly* said *exactly* what he was analogizing: people would be caught up in their daily lives and not take heed to the warning of judgment coming. That's it. He indicated nothing beyond that single purpose of the image. The point was to be watchful and ready for coming judgment, not to watch for Nephilim and genetic hybridization.

"But wait!" says the futurist Nephilim theorist, "Jesus said, 'In those days before the flood, they were marrying and giving in marriage!' That is a reference to the sons of God marrying daughters of men in Genesis 6:2."

But if you read Jesus' words in context, it is clearly *not* a reference to that peculiar instance of species intermarriage.

> Matthew 24:38–39
> For as in those days before the flood they were eating and drinking, marrying and giving in marriage, until the day when Noah entered the ark, [39] and they were unaware until the flood came and swept them all away, so will be the coming of the Son of Man.

Do we then speculate that when Jesus said that "they were eating and drinking" that he meant the giants were eating humans and drinking their blood? (1 Enoch 7:2-5). No doubt, some do. But you can see how such unfettered allegorizing becomes a license for all kinds of ridiculous speculation. Text without context is pretext. Jesus was not referring to the unique situation of angelic-human sexual intercourse; he was referring to *normal* eating and drinking and *normal* marriage in the *normal* context of *normal* lives that people were living. They just went on with their normal lives instead of heeding the warning. To import the breeding of Nephilim through angelic-human intercourse into Jesus' words is to force an alien intent onto the text that is at odds with Jesus' stated intent. So much damage has been done to the spiritual welfare of the body of Christ through this kind of twisting of Scripture out of its intended context.

And in A.D. 70, those who did not heed Jesus' words and continued on with their lives in Israel were swept away in the judgment—just like Jesus predicted. Those Christians who listened to Jesus fled to Pella to avoid the slaughter, as we already indicated in chapter 11.

The Rapture?

The very next thing that Jesus talked about in relation to his coming was the image of people being separated during the judgment.

> Matthew 24:39–42
> [A]nd they were unaware until the flood came and swept them all away, so will be the coming of the Son of Man. [40] Then two men will be in the field; one will be taken and one left. [41] Two women will be grinding at the mill; one will be taken and one left. [42] Therefore, stay awake, for you do not know on what day your Lord is coming.

Those who believe in a rapture think that this is a depiction of the rapture. Since they believe that the rapture will come and surprise us, they picture the common *Left Behind* scenario of plane loads of people crashing to the ground as Christian pilots are raptured into heaven. Isn't that what Jesus meant when he said, "One will be taken and one left [behind]"?

Those who believe this is a reference to the rapture have some pretty insurmountable problems that they have backed themselves into.

First of all, this event is described as part of the single coming of the Son of Man. It is not a first stage, secret coming, where Jesus comes in the sky, raptures Christians, and goes back to heaven to come back again seven years later. The text does not describe two comings. There is one, single coming of the Son of Man.

Secondly, the picture of "being taken" is not one of the "rapture of the righteous" but a picture of captivity. As we've already pointed out historically and biblically, exile and captivity was God's means of separating people in Israel during periods of judgment for disobedience toward him.

Think about it: Noah and his family were left behind. It was the rest of humanity that was taken away in judgment.

When the first Jerusalem temple was destroyed in 586 B.C., the separation of people in exile was described in these same exact terms that Jesus used in Matthew 24. And it would make sense that he would use the same imagery, because he was describing a similar destruction of the temple and exile for the Jews.

> Jeremiah 6:11–12
> Therefore I am full of the wrath of the LORD; I am weary of holding it in. "Pour it out upon the children in the street, and upon the gatherings of young men, also; both husband and wife shall be taken, the elderly and the very aged. [12] Their houses shall be turned over to others, their fields and wives together, for I will stretch out my hand against the inhabitants of the land," declares the LORD.

The Jewish historian Josephus wrote about the A.D. 70 destruction with the same terminology that Jesus used, in describing those taken away in captivity versus those who were "left behind."

> Josephus, Wars, 6:8:2 (6.384-386)
> [The Romans] left only the populace [of Jerusalem], and sold the rest of the multitude, with their wives and children, and every one of them at a very low price… (386) and indeed the number of those that were sold was immense; but of the populace above forty thousand were saved, whom Caesar let go whither every one of them pleased.[1]

[1] Flavius Josephus and William Whiston, *The Works of Josephus: Complete and Unabridged* (Peabody: Hendrickson, 1987).

> Josephus, Wars, 6:9:3 (6.420-421)
> Now the number of those that were carried captive during this whole war was collected to be ninety-seven thousand; as was the number of those that perished during the whole siege eleven hundred thousand, (421) the greater part of whom were indeed of the same nation [with the citizens of Jerusalem], but not belonging to the city itself.[2]

Jesus was not coming to rapture Christians; he was coming in judgment to take away into captivity those who rejected him, while leaving his elect (Christians) safely hidden in the mountains to return to their lives and spread the gospel of the kingdom.

Does this mean that no Christians were killed in the judgment on Jerusalem or that *all* Christians fled to the mountains in obedience to Jesus? Of course not. Such absolute thinking is a product of modern scientific precision and has no place in biblical interpretation. Yes, God spared all the righteous from Sodom before destroying it, but he did not spare all the righteous when the first temple was destroyed in 586 B.C. and Israel judged. Daniel, Isaiah, Ezekiel, and others would beg to differ with those who would seek to say that there were no righteous Jews in captivity during the Assyrian or Babylonian exile.

The separation of men in the field and women at the mill in Matthew 24:40-41 is a separation of captivity for those who stayed in Jerusalem while Rome descended upon her for destruction in A.D. 70. They should have heeded Jesus' words.

A Thief in the Night

I remember way back in the 1970s, when I first saw what could very well be the first Christian narrative movie about the end times, *A Thief in the Night*. It was a low, low budget movie version of *Left Behind*, long before *Left Behind*. It became a standard of (bad) Christian writing, directing, and acting for generations to come. It began with Christians disappearing in a rapture, leaving people to face a one-world government that would hunt

[2] Flavius Josephus and William Whiston, *The Works of Josephus: Complete and Unabridged* (Peabody: Hendrickson, 1987).

down people who became believers and lead them to United Nations guillotines.

Unfortunately, this understanding of the "thief in the night" as the rapture is another gross misunderstanding based on taking the verse out of its ancient context. The stated theme of Jesus' parable was a thief *judging the unprepared*, not a *rapturing of believers* before a second coming.

> Matthew 24:43–44
> But know this, that if the master of the house had known in what part of the night the thief was coming, he would have stayed awake and would not have let his house be broken into. [44] Therefore you also must be ready, for the Son of Man is coming at an hour you do not expect.

The Wise and Wicked Servants

The last parable that Jesus used to emphasize readiness for judgment is undeniably an affirmation of everything in the section, since he used the same language of coming "on a day when he does not expect him and at an hour he does not know." So this is a fourfold repetition of a theme in four images; the fig tree, the days of Noah, the thief in the night, and now the wise and wicked servants.

> Matthew 24:45–51
> Who then is the faithful and wise servant, whom his master has set over his household, to give them their food at the proper time? [46] Blessed is that servant whom his master will find so doing when he comes. [47] Truly, I say to you, he will set him over all his possessions. [48] But if that wicked servant says to himself, "My master is delayed," [49] and begins to beat his fellow servants and eats and drinks with drunkards, [50] the master of that servant will come on a day when he does not expect him and at an hour he does not know [51] and will cut him in pieces and put him with the hypocrites. In that place there will be weeping and gnashing of teeth.

This fourth reference to the surprising nearness of the coming of the Son of Man means that this parable—usually misinterpreted by Christians to be a parable of the second coming of Christ—is actually a parable of his first coming in judgment in A.D. 70. Like the parable of the vineyard that warned the Jews of God coming to them in judgment for rejecting Messiah (Matt 21:42-44), this parable also reinforced that same warning that the Jews were wicked servants in God's kingdom who did not fulfill their duty, but instead became wicked and beat their "fellow servants," the Christians and prophets of Matthew 23:30-36 and 24:9.

This same language of "the master delayed" and "thief in the night" and "days of Noah" was also used by the apostle Peter in his admonition to Christians of his era to be patient in the light of an apparent delay in Christ's coming. In fact, Peter used all the imagery we have been writing about—the day of the Lord, heavens and earth, cosmic catastrophe. Now that the reader is familiar with this poetic language, a rereading of 2 Peter 3 will yield a much different picture than the typical one of most futurists. Since that is a bit of a tangent from Matthew 24, I have included an appendix at the back of this book about "The Day of the Lord in 2 Peter."

Peter, Paul, and the other writers of the New Testament letters were not telling Christians to be patient because Jesus was coming in thousands of years, but to be patient because his coming was "near," "soon," "at hand," "right at the door," and "within this generation" of those living at the time of Jesus.

Chapter 16
But What about…?

The paradigm of interpretation I have expressed in this book is no doubt a shocking one for many readers. And if you are anything like me, when you are first introduced to this new way of seeing prophecy, you may react with revulsion or fear of heresy. I did. After all, you have most likely been taught the predominant, futurist view of the end times and the only disagreements you may consider valid are whether a rapture comes pre-trib, mid-trib or post-trib, or whether the mark of the Beast is a computer implant or a genetic splice. To suggest that the abomination of desolation, the Beast and his mark, the great tribulation and the coming of the Son of Man occurred in the first century is to shake the very core of the futurist's assumed beliefs.

Such shaking of our "heavens and earth" is uncomfortable, even frightening. And no doubt there are many Bible passages you've been taught that pop into your head that seem at odds with this understanding. For example, What about Ezekiel 38 and 39? What about Revelation? What about Daniel? What about the new heavens and earth? What about . . .? (fill in the blank with your most beloved Bible prophecy passage)

The same thing happened to me. And those questions are legitimate and demand answers. But it takes time to reinterpret an entire system of beliefs within a new paradigm. Have patience. I don't have the space to address all those questions here. But there are answers for all the questions. I only wanted to establish a solid foundation for the need of a new paradigm. So I have provided a bibliography of books with this preterist interpretation at the back of this book. Those are wiser men than I am, scholars who address all those questions with a high view of Scripture, high credentials and a high standard of biblical proof. Take the next step and explore an exciting world of biblical poetry and imagination that gives meaning to the new covenant of Jesus Christ in ways you have only begun to appreciate.

Double Fulfillment

A common reaction that occurs when faced with this evidence of the first century fulfillment of end times prophecy is an appeal to double fulfillment of prophecy, also called "double reference." This means that a prophecy may refer to two different kinds of fulfillment: one close to the time period of the prophecy and one distant in time from the original prediction. This double fulfillment notion results in the claim that maybe the prophecies of the coming of the Son of Man in the last days were fulfilled in the first century, but they will also be fulfilled again in our future with the physical return of Christ. In other words, the prophecies are fulfilled twice in two different comings of the Son of Man.

This understanding of double fulfillment is quite complicated and continues to be debated among the finest of scholars and theologians, without definitive conclusions on either side. I am not going to solve this hermeneutical debate in my one measly chapter. My only goal is to suggest some reasons why I think that, despite its tempting offer to have the best of both worlds of eschatology, the double fulfillment theory ultimately creates more problems than it solves and fails to deliver a satisfactory interpretation of prophecy fulfillment.

The Upside of Double Fulfillment

The first thing that double fulfillment has going for it is that prophetic interpretation in the New Testament is somewhat loose and flexible. It doesn't tend to adhere to the kind of fundamentalist, rigid precision that some Bible interpreters would prefer, especially when it comes to messianic fulfillment. There are some prophecies that are literally predicted and fulfilled, such as the Bethlehem birth of Messiah (Mic 5:2, fulfilled in Matt 2:1-6). But there are also some prophecies where the New Testament writers changed a word in the original prophecy (Eph 3:8 "gave gifts" vs. Psa 68:18 "received gifts"), others that are symbolic fulfillments (Mal 4:5-6 vs. Matt 11:13-14), and many others where the prophecy is not really a deliberate prophecy at all, but a typological connection (Matt 2:5 vs. Hos 11:1). So I will readily admit that we must be careful not to force our scientific precision upon an ancient understanding of prophecy.

Appeal is often made to the claim that the messianic prophecies of the Old Testament had double fulfillment, so why can't the Matthew 24 prophecies have double fulfillment? For example, the prophecy of the "virgin with child," in Isaiah 7:14 had both a local referent in King Ahaz's child and a distant fulfillment in Jesus (Matt 1:23). But this is not a certain interpretation, by any means. There are many scholars who argue that the promise of Messiah in Isaiah is a growing picture that includes the eternal, deified throne of David (Isa 9), and the branch of Jesse yet to bring the new covenant (Isa 11), and many other elements clearly not fulfilled in Ahaz's child or any other local referent of that time period. An entire tradition of interpretation still carries weight that messianic prophecies were fulfilled in the lone person of Jesus Christ, without a double reference.

But I am not wed to this tradition either. There is too much ambiguity in prophecy to claim absolute knowledge of interpretation. But even if there is a double fulfillment of prophecy, it still becomes problematic when trying to apply it to Matthew 24 and the coming of the Son of Man. I'll tell you why.

The Downside of Double Fulfillment

First, we have already seen that Jesus' prophecies were so specifically fulfilled in the first century in all their details that, on the face of things, there is no indication of any kind of future double fulfillment. Indeed, there is no need for a second fulfillment. The text simply doesn't read that way. If everything was fulfilled, there is nothing left to be fulfilled.

Second, if you appeal to double fulfillment for prophecies, what becomes your criteria for applying that interpretation? Is *every prophecy* doubly fulfilled? If not, why not? Why would there not also be a double Elijah beyond John the Baptist? And if Messiah was born once in Bethlehem, do you believe another future Messiah might be born there in double fulfillment? Do you believe that another Messiah may die for our sins in double fulfillment? I sure hope not. The answer to these challenges lies in an appeal to the finality of the messianic office. His death was "once for all" so he would not need to die again. Once Messiah came, the old covenant was gone forever, replaced by the new covenant. Final completion of messianic atonement in-and-of-itself discredits a future double fulfillment for messianic prophecy.

But that is precisely why double fulfillment fails to apply to a future judgment upon Jerusalem beyond the first century. The prophecies of God's judgment upon Jerusalem and the temple in Matthew 23 and 24 were also final and absolute as well. Remember all those statements by Jesus of the finality of judgment upon the final generation that rejected Messiah? Once the temple was destroyed and replaced by the new covenant body of Christ as the temple, there would be no need for another physical temple. Jesus is the new temple once for all, just like his death was once for all. The new covenant marks the final rejection of unbelieving Jews and the handing over of the kingdom to a new people who would produce the fruit. There cannot be a final rejection after the final rejection has already occurred. If the judgment of the temple and city marked the end of the old covenant and the start of the new covenant, it would be evidently ludicrous to suggest that there will be another "newer" new covenant all over again. There can be no double fulfillment of the end of the old covenant age.

Thirdly, even if you accept the double fulfillment theory, you would have to acknowledge that Jesus' prophecy in the Olivet Discourse *was* the double fulfillment, not the first fulfillment. Remember, Jesus was reiterating Daniel's abomination of desolation (Dan 9) and the Son of Man coming on the clouds (Dan 7). The destruction of Jerusalem and the temple in A.D. 70 was already the second occurrence of such a thing in history, not the first. So in order to argue that Jesus' prophecy of destruction referred to a distant judgment is to argue for a third fulfillment, not a double fulfillment. But if there are three fulfillments, why aren't there four? You can see how this approach reduces to the absurdity of arbitrary speculation or the personal whims of the interpreter.

I can only conclude that in light of the problems that double fulfillment raises, it is apparent that its adoption lay in the unwillingness to give up cherished preconceptions in the light of new evidence. When you *assume* an unfulfilled worldwide prophecy of the future and then see that prophecy fulfilled in a local historical event, you must reconfigure your web of beliefs to maintain the old belief while adding the evidence for the new belief by creating the double fulfillment theory. You might call this having your theological cake and eating it too. But, unfortunately for the believer in double fulfillment, it doesn't fit the text or the context of Jesus' Olivet Discourse. It remains a pretext.

Typological Fulfillment

Some light may be shed on the matter by understanding the nature of typological fulfillment of prophecy. What many people think are double fulfillments are actually not double references at all, but *typological* fulfillments. This means that God's prophetic discourse through the scriptures is sometimes an ongoing repetition of certain images ("types") that find their ultimate, climactic fulfillment in the final "antitype" of Christ. Another way of describing typological fulfillment is the term "foreshadowing." Types foreshadow the final antitype.

For example, the promise in Genesis 3:15 that the messianic seed or offspring would crush the head of the serpent's offspring is foreshadowed over and over again throughout the Old Testament as a meme of this battle.

- David (the "anointed one") crushed Goliath's skull with his stone (1 Sam 17:49).
- God crushed the skulls of Canaanites in the Promised Land (Psa 68:21).
- Messiah would be "crushed for our sins" (Isa 53:5).
- Jael killed Israel's enemy Sisera by crushing his skull with a tent peg (Judg 4:21)
- Jesus' death on the cross took place on Golgotha, "Place of the Skull" and a word derived from Goliath (Matt 27:33).

The skull crushing by the messianic seed line was not multiple fulfillments, but rather typological foreshadowing of the repetitious image. In the same way, the abomination of desolation was also an image that generically represented anything at any time that defiled God's holy place. Rather than being a specific prediction of an individual, Daniel described the armies of Antiochus Epiphanes as an abomination of desolation (Dan 11:31; 1Macc. 1:34–35), and then he prophesied about Titus and his Roman armies of abomination that would bring desolation (Dan 9:27; Luke 21:20). These were not two fulfillments of one abomination of desolation, but rather one typological term that was used in two different prophecies. The abomination of desolation is a generic type, not a specific double fulfillment.

This applies to the phrase "coming of the Son of Man," which we already saw could occur in multiple comings. There were not multiple fulfillments; but rather whenever God came in judgment on a city or nation, he used the same imagery of "coming on the clouds" to express his glory and power in judgment. So when Jesus came in glory and powerful judgment on Israel in the first century, that was simply the use of a common expression and not a double fulfillment. When he comes physically a second time, that will not be a double fulfillment of the AD 70 coming, but simply a different and final coming of many comings that God has performed.

The idea of typological fulfillment of prophecy is another rich excursion into fascinating Bible study that warrants a book by itself. I will leave the reader with this brief introduction with the challenge for more research.

Postponed Fulfillment?

Another way of interpreting the Olivet Discourse in light of futurist assumptions is through postponed fulfillment. The argument proposes that prophetic declarations of judgment by God are always contingent upon human response. That is, if God says he is going to destroy a city or nation and they repent, he is not obligated to follow through with his promise. Human repentance changes the equation. God said this quite explicitly to Jeremiah.

> Jeremiah 18:7–10
> If at any time I declare concerning a nation or a kingdom, that I will pluck up and break down and destroy it, [8] and if that nation, concerning which I have spoken, turns from its evil, I will relent of the disaster that I intended to do to it. [9] And if at any time I declare concerning a nation or a kingdom that I will build and plant it, [10] and if it does evil in my sight, not listening to my voice, then I will relent of the good that I had intended to do to it.

This is why Nineveh was not judged even though God told Jonah to preach its downfall. When people repent, God may stop or delay his judgment. And conversely, if people become wicked, God may judge where he said he wouldn't. Therefore, if God doesn't follow through with a prophecy, that doesn't mean he won't follow through at a later date. Daniel exemplified this alteration of prophetic judgment when he said that Jeremiah's original prophecy of seventy years of desolation was extended and became seventy weeks of years before God would bring redemption (Dan 9:2, 24). God postponed the coming of Messiah for over 400 years past the original prophecy of Jeremiah.

This postponement theory is then invoked for Matthew 24 to explain why it hasn't been fulfilled yet. Unfortunately, for the postponement view, it can't apply to Matthew 24 for several reasons.

First, this book has already shown that every element of the prophecy was in fact biblically fulfilled, even the coming of the Son of Man. So there is no evidence in the text or in history for postponement. You can't say something has been postponed when it has already happened.

Secondly, the Olivet Discourse was a prophecy of judgment upon Jews for rejecting Messiah. The fact that the temple was destroyed as Jesus said proves that they did not repent as a nation. God judged them as he said he would. They didn't repent as did the city of Nineveh. There was no human response that changed Jesus' prophecy.

The postponement theory of prophecy just doesn't apply to the judgment of A.D. 70 because nothing was postponed! Jesus said he would come in judgment and destroy the temple, and he did. Postponement may calm the fretful heart of the futurist desperate to justify his eschatology, but it just doesn't fit the facts of biblical history.

Conclusion

At this point, I would like to recommend my novel series, *Chronicles of the Apocalypse*, for further exploration of this preterist approach to the end times. In that series I tell the story of the events that led up to the destruction of Jerusalem and the temple in A.D. 70. And I show the spiritual machinations hinted at in the book of Revelation. I incarnate the meaning of the symbols in Revelation in historical dramatic narrative. This makes them come alive in a way that theological texts cannot achieve. Perhaps this is why the end times novel series *Left Behind* captivated so many minds and hearts. When you see the theology incarnated through historical dramatic narrative, you see the big picture in a way that is more captivating than the fine details of systematic theology. Through story, you inhabit the theology and connect with the meaning in a deeper way than mere intellectual assent.

So check out Chronicles of the Apocalypse for the fuller treatment of this understanding of end times Bible prophecy, since it's not what they told you.

Appendix
The Day of the Lord in 2 Peter

> 2 Pet. 3:10–13
> But the day of the Lord will come like a thief, and then the heavens will pass away with a roar, and the elements will be burned up and dissolved, and the earth and the works that are done on it will be exposed…
>
> Since all these things are thus to be dissolved, what sort of people ought you to be in lives of holiness and godliness, waiting for and hastening the coming of the day of God, because of which the heavens will be set on fire and dissolved, and the elements will melt as they burn! But according to His promise we are waiting for new heavens and a new earth in which righteousness dwells.

The interpretation I have presented in this book is no doubt earth shattering for some eschatological paradigms about the end times. Such radical departures from the futurist's perceived wisdom always begs plenty of questions about other passages and concepts taken for granted by the futurist interpretation.

One passage is the apparently clear description in 2 Peter about the day of the Lord and the passing away of the heavens and the earth that are replaced by a new heavens and earth. Isn't that unambiguous language to be taken literally? Well, actually, no. As a matter of fact, orthodox believers have wide-ranging interpretations of this passage, so it is a controversial one to begin with.[1]

---

[1] Bauckham, Richard J. Vol. 50, *Word Biblical Commentary: 2 Peter, Jude*. Word Biblical Commentary. Dallas: Word, Incorporated, 2002, p. 315-319.

We must remember our dictum to seek to understand the text within its ancient Jewish setting steeped in Old Testament imagery and symbols. I believe when we do this, we will have to conclude that the decreation of the heavens and earth is covenantal mythopoeia, *not* literal, physical, scientific observation. Peter wrote figuratively about the final ending of the old covenant, with God's judgment on Israel for rejecting Messiah and the final establishment of his new covenant as a new world order, or, in their case, a "new heavens and new earth."

In the beginning of chapter 3, Peter compared the scoffers of his day and their impending judgment with the scoffers of Noah's day before their judgment. The judgment was near; and, what's more, these scoffers were in the last days, which we have already seen were considered the last days of the old covenant that the New Testament writers were living in. Those last days would be climaxed by judgment. But what kind of judgment?

Peter referenced the creation of the heavens and earth (red flag about covenants!) and then the destruction of that previous world by water. Scholars have indicated how the flood of Noah was described using terms similar to Genesis 1, as if God was "decreating" the earth because of sin, in order to start over with a new Noahic covenant.[2] The ark floated over the chaotic "face of the waters" (Gen 7:17), just as God's spirit had hovered over the chaotic face of the waters before creation (Gen 1:2). The dry land receded from the waters (8:3), just as it had been separated in creation (1:9). God gave the command to Noah to be fruitful and multiply and fill the earth (9:1), just as he had given it to Adam and Eve (1:28). So the covenantal connections are loud and clear.

As already noted, the day of the Lord is always used in the Bible for a localized judgment upon a people, which, by way of reminder, Jesus had already prophesied was coming upon Jerusalem to the very generation he spoke to (Matt. 23:36-24:2). But what makes some interpreters think this is the final judgment of the universe is the very bad translation of the Greek word *stoicheion* as "elements" in some English texts. This makes modern readers think of the periodic table of elements as being the most foundational

---

[2]Wenham, Gordon J. Vol. 1, *Word Biblical Commentary: Genesis 1-15*. Word Biblical Commentary. Dallas: Word, Incorporated, 2002, p. 207.

building blocks of the universe. They conclude that the Bible must be talking about the actual elements of helium, hydrogen, deuterium, and others being burned up and melted!

But this is not what the Greek word means. Though some Greek thinkers believed in the existence of atoms, the common understanding was that there were four basic elements—earth, water, wind, and fire.[3] Though someone may conjecture that these could still be considered physical elements that could be destroyed, a simple look at the usage of *stoicheion* throughout the New Testament shows that the Hebrew usage had nothing to do with Greek primitive scientific notions.

In every place that *stoicheion* shows up in the New Testament it refers to elementary principles of a worldview, sometimes a godless worldview (Col 2:8), but, more often, the elementary principles of the old covenant law described as a "cosmos" (Gal 4:3, 9; Col 2:20; Heb 5:12).[4]

Remember how the cosmic language of creating heavens and earth was used to describe the cosmic significance of God establishing a covenant? And remember how in the Old Testament, the destruction of covenants, nations, and peoples was described in *decreation* terms as the collapsing of the universe?

That is the case in these passages as well, with the term "cosmos" being used metaphorically for the "universe" of God's covenantal order as embodied in the old covenant laws of Jewish separation: circumcision, dietary restrictions, and sabbaths. Paul was telling his readers that the *stoicheion* of the old covenant *cosmos* were no longer over them because the people of God were under new *stoicheion*, the elementary principles of faith (Gal 4:1-11).

Peter meant the same thing. When he said that the heavens will pass away and the *stoicheion* will be burned up, he was claiming that when the

---

[3] Schreiner, Thomas R. Vol. 37, *1, 2 Peter, Jude*. electronic ed. Logos Library System; The New American Commentary. Nashville: Broadman & Holman Publishers, 2007, p. 384.

[4] Leithart, Peter J. *The Promise of His Appearing: An Exposition of Second Peter*. Moscow, ID: Canon Press, 2004, p.101. Bauckham argues that "The heavenly bodies (sun, moon and stars) is the interpretation favored by most commentators," for *stoicheion*. But then we are right back to the sun, moon, and stars as figurative language of covenantal elements. Bauckham, *2 Peter, Jude*, 316. But I doubt this interpretation because the clear words for "heavenly bodies" are not *stoicheion*, but *epouranios soma* (1 Cor. 15:40-41).

temple in Jerusalem is destroyed, it will be the final passing away of the old covenant cosmos. This would include all the elementary principles tied to that physical sacramental structure—the laws that once separated Jew and Gentile. The new cosmos would be one in which both Jew and Gentile "by God's power are being guarded through faith for a salvation ready to be revealed in the last time" (1 Pet 1:5).

As Gary DeMar concluded, "The New Covenant replaces the Old Covenant with new leaders, a new priesthood, new sacraments, a new sacrifice, a new tabernacle (John 1:14), and a new temple (John 2:19; 1 Cor. 3:16; Eph. 2:21). In essence, a new heaven and earth."[5] Eminent Greek scholar John Lightfoot agreed, "The destruction of Jerusalem and the whole Jewish state is described as if the whole frame of this world were to be dissolved."[6] Kenneth Gentry adds, "'The temple was more than a building and more than the home of the sacrificial cult. It was the sacred center of the cosmos, the place where heaven and earth meet.' Thus, the collapse of the temple becomes a picture of the end of Israel's world, her covenantal universe."[7]

The new heavens and new earth in which righteousness dwells that Peter was waiting for was the new covenant cosmos of righteousness by faith inaugurated by Christ's death and resurrection. That new covenant inauguration and implementation was not merely an abstract claim of contractual change, it was physically verified with the destruction of the old covenant emblem, the temple, that finalized the dissolution of the old covenant itself.

> Matt. 23:36-38
> "O Jerusalem, Jerusalem, the city that kills the prophets and stones those who are sent to it! How often would I have gathered your children together as a hen gathers her brood under her wings, and you would not! See, your house [temple] is left to you desolate. Truly, I say to you, all these things will come upon this generation.

---

[5] Gary DeMar, *Last Days Madness*, p. 192.
[6] Lightfoot, John. *Commentary on the New Testament from the Talmud and Hebraica: Matthew – 1 Corinthians*, 4 vols. Peabody, MA: Hendrickson, 1859, 1989, 3:454.
[7] Kenneth L. Gentry, Jr., *The Divorce of Israel: A Redemptive-Historical Interpretation of Revelation*, (Dallas, GA: Tolle Lege Press, 2016), 63.

Want More of this Fascinating Research?

Sign up Online For The Godawa Chronicles

http://www.godawa.com

Insider information on the novels of Brian Godawa,
Special Discounts! Free Articles!
Cool Artwork and Videos!

GET THIS FREE eBOOK!

Limited Time Offer

FREE

The Research Behind This Book That You Are Now Reading

By Brian Godawa

100 pages of biblical and historical sources, with citations proving the fulfillment of each verse in Matthew 24. PDF format.

http://godawa.com/matthew-24/

About The Author

Brian Godawa is the screenwriter for the award-winning feature film, *To End All Wars,* starring Kiefer Sutherland. It was awarded the Commander in Chief Medal of Service, Honor and Pride by the Veterans of Foreign Wars, won the first Heartland Film Festival by storm, and showcased the Cannes Film Festival Cinema for Peace.

He also co-wrote *Alleged*, starring Brian Dennehy as Clarence Darrow and Fred Thompson as William Jennings Bryan. He previously adapted to film the best-selling supernatural thriller novel *The Visitation* by author Frank Peretti for Ralph Winter (*X-Men, Wolverine*), and wrote and directed *Wall of Separation,* a PBS documentary, and *Lines That Divide*, a documentary on stem cell research.

Mr. Godawa's scripts have won multiple awards in respected screenplay competitions, and his articles on movies and philosophy have been published around the world. He has traveled around the United States teaching on movies, worldviews, and culture to colleges, churches and community groups.

His popular book, *Hollywood Worldviews: Watching Films with Wisdom and Discernment* (InterVarsity Press) is used as a textbook in schools around the country. His novel series, the saga *Chronicles of the Nephilim* is in the Top 10 of Biblical Fiction on Amazon and is an imaginative retelling of Biblical stories of the Nephilim giants, the secret plan of the fallen Watchers, and the War of the Seed of the Serpent with the Seed of Eve. The sequel series, *Chronicles of the Apocalypse* tells the story of the Apostle John's book of Revelation, and *Chronicles of the Watchers* recounts true history through the Watcher paradigm.

Find out more about his other books, lecture tapes and dvds for sale at his website **www.godawa.com**.

Bibliography of Books on Bible Prophecy from A Preterist Perspective

For additional Biblical and historical research related to this series, go to www.ChroniclesoftheApocalypse.com and Click on Scholarly Research.

John L. Bray, *Matthew 24 Fulfilled*, (American Vision; 5th Edition, 2009).

David Chilton, *The Days of Vengeance: An Exposition of the Book of Revelation*, (Dominion Press; 1st Edition, 2006).

Gary DeMar, *10 Popular Prophecy Myths Exposed: The Last Days Might Not Be as Near as You Think*, (American Vision, 2010).

— *Last Days Madness: Obsession of the Modern Church* Wolgemuth & Hyatt Pub; 4th Revised edition (September 1999).

— *Left Behind: Separating Fact From Fiction*, (American Vision; First edition, 2010).

— *Why the End of the World is Not in Your Future: Identifying the Gog-Magog Alliance*, (American Vision; First edition, 2010)

Kenneth L. Gentry, Jr., *The Beast of Revelation*, (American Vision, 2002).

— *Before Jerusalem Fell: Dating the Book of Revelation*, (Victorious Hope Publishing, 2010)

— *The Book of Revelation Made Easy: You Can Understand Bible Prophecy*, American Vision (December 31, 2009).

— *The Divorce of Israel: A Redemptive-Historical Interpretation of Revelation Vol. 1 & 2*, (Liberty Alliance, 2016).

— *Navigating the Book of Revelation: Special Studies on Important Issues*, (GoodBirth Ministries, 2011).

— *The Olivet Discourse Made Easy*, (Apologetics Group. 2010)

— *Perilous Times: A Study in Eschatological Evil*, (Covenant Media Press, 1999).

Kenneth L. Gentry Jr., and Thomas Ice, *The Great Tribulation: Past or Future?: Two Evangelicals Debate the Question*, (Kregel Academic & Professional, 1999).

John H. Gerstner, *Wrongly Dividing the Word of Truth: A Critique of Dispensationalism 3rd Edition* (Nicene Council, 2009).

Hank Hanegraaff, *The Apocalypse Code: Find out What the Bible Really Says About the End Times and Why It Matters Today,* (Thomas Nelson, 2010).

George Peter Holford, *The Destruction of Jerusalem: An Absolute and Irresistible Proof of the Divine Origin of Christianity*, (Covenant Media Press; 6th American edition, 2001).

Peter J. Leithart, *The Promise of His Appearing: An Exposition of Second Peter* (Canon Press, 2004).

Keith A. Mathison, *Dispensationalism: Rightly Dividing the People of God?* (P & R Publishing, 1995).

Philip Mauro, *The Seventy Weeks and the Great Tribulation: A Study of the Last Two Visions of Daniel and the Olivet Discourse of the Lord Jesus Christ* (Hamilton Brothers, 1922).

R.C. Sproul, *The Last Days According to Jesus: When Did Jesus Say He Would Return? 2nd Edition,* (Baker Pub Group, 1998).

Get More Biblical Imagination

Sign up Online For The Godawa Chronicles

www.Godawa.com

Insider information on the novels of Brian Godawa
Special Discounts, New Releases,
Bible Mysteries!
We won't spam you.

Are We Living in the Last Days?

Check out this Controversial Online Course!

25% OFF!

Limited Time Only

10+ Intense Lectures on End Times

Powerpoint Videos with Powerful Visuals By Brian Godawa

There are so many Christians teaching outrageous things about Bible Prophecy these days. It's enough to frustrate the serious Bible student. What would you think if you found out most all of it is simply mistaken? What if you found out that the ancient mindset of the Jewish writers was influenced by the Old Testament imagery of the past, and not a crystal ball gaze into our modern future? What if you found out that everything that modern prophecy pundits are looking for—the antichrist, the Beast, the Tribulation, the Rapture—was not what they told you it was, but something different?

Includes lots of colorful and helpful PowerPoint visuals, charts, pictures, and film clips for a much richer presentation of the material.

PLUS a bunch of FREE Bonuses!

Check out the Free Introduction & Learn More
(Use Code NTBA84 for 25% Discount)

Click Here For Details

LastDaysCourse.com

Chronicles of the Apocalypse

A Novel Series About the Book of Revelation & the End Times. A Fresh Biblical View.

www.Godawa.com

Chronicles of the Nephilim

Nephilim Giants, Watchers, Cosmic War.
All in the Bible. Now in Novels.

www.Godawa.com

Chronicles of the Watchers

A Series About the Watchers in History.
Action, Romance, Gods, Monsters & Men.

The first novel is *The Dragon King: First Emperor of China*

www.Godawa.com

Get Lectures by Brian Godawa
Audio & Video Online Downloads

GODAWA.COM
(Click on Store)

Audio & Video Lectures on Art, Movies, Faith and Worldviews

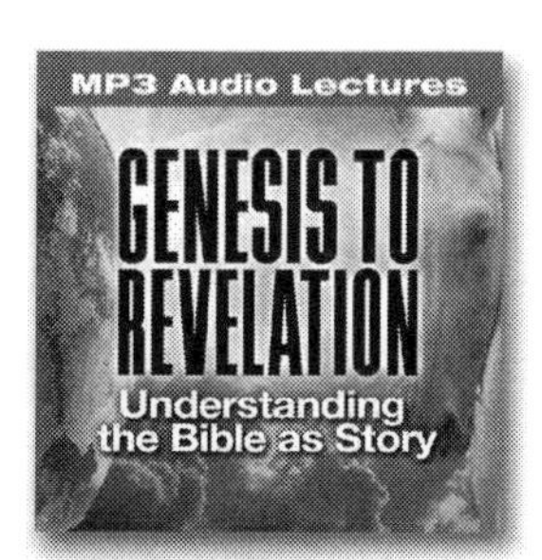

WWW.GODAWA.COM/STORE

Made in the USA
Lexington, KY
12 February 2019